Hamden Public Library

P9-CER-551

31200500078083

MILLER LIBRARY
2901 DIXWELL AVE.
HAMDEN, CT 06518

DATE

JUL 9 2015

7 Steps to
Spiritual
Intelligence

MILLER LIBRARY
2901 DIXWELL AVE.
HAMDEN, CT 06518

BASED ON CLASSICAL ISLAMIC TEACHINGS

7 *Steps to Spiritual Intelligence*

Musharraf Hussain

KUBE
PUBLISHING

7 Steps to Spiritual Intelligence

First published in England by Kube Publishing Ltd.
Markfield Conference Centre
Ratby Lane, Markfield,
Leicestershire LE67 9SY
United Kingdom
Tel: +44 (0)1530 249230
Fax: +44 (0)1530 249656
Website: www.kubepublishing.com
Email: info@kubepubishing.com

© Musharraf Hussain, 2014
All rights reserved

The right of Musharraf Hussain to be identified
as the author of this work has been asserted by him
in accordance with the Copyright, Designs and
Patents Act, 1988.

CIP data for this book is available from the British Library.

ISBN 978-1-84774-078-6 *paperback*
ISBN 978-1-84774-xxx-x *ebook*

Cover design: Nasir Cadir
Book design and typesetting: Nasir Cadir

Printed by IMAK Ofset, Turkey

MILLER LIBRARY
2901 DIXWELL AVE
HAMDEN, CT 06518

In the name of God, Most Gracious, Most Compassionate

Contents

MILLER LIBRARY
2901 DIXWELL AVE.
HAMDEN, CT 06518

Preface

A noteworthy human characteristic is curiosity about the mysteries of nature, of our own nature and the big questions of life: Where have I come from? Where am I going? And what is the meaning and purpose of life? Spiritual intelligence provides the most convincing and practical response to these questions.

For Muslims, the first source of spiritual intelligence is the glorious Qur'an; every verse is a constant reminder of God's benevolence, wisdom and power. This handbook aims to explain simply and rationally the nature and scope of spiritual intelligence and its key elements. The purpose of spiritual intelligence is to gain a deeper understanding of God, thereby attaining peace of mind. It is to renew the heart so that one begins to live with God.

The second source is the life example of our beloved Messenger ﷺ. Whilst the Qur'an guides us with God's teachings, the blessed Messenger ﷺ is a living example for us, a universal role model for the believer seeking God. Through him, we gain inspiration by following his prayer, fasting and remembrance of God, his vigils at night, his solitude and silence, all reflecting his spiritual intimacy with God.

This handbook also summarizes fourteen centuries of spiritual wisdom in Islamic literature, from which I have plucked ripe and succulent fruits from the great teachers, scholars and Sufis of Spain, Morocco, Turkey and India. I have endeavoured to present their teachings in a contemporary language and style, and you will be the best judges of how successful I have been in doing so.

I am grateful to Yahya Birt, Kube's Commissioning Editor, for his constant encouragement in undertaking this wonderful journey, and to my daughter Nabeela Khan for her help with the manuscript. Finally, I pray that Allah Most Gracious accepts my humble efforts and makes the quest for spiritual intelligence easy for you and me.

Musharraf Hussain
Nottingham
June 2014

Chapter One

The Meaning and Scope of Spiritual Intelligence

In affluent societies, both East and West, surveys repeatedly show that people are surprisingly unhappy. The apparent joys of consumerism, consumption and material wealth in the affluent society mask the shallowness of worldly life. A young man told me, 'I've got emptiness deep inside,' as he described his feelings; others often tell me that they have 'a deep void' or that 'a chunk is missing from my soul'. Linked with today's materialism is celebrity culture, which replaces true role models with movie stars, singers and footballers. One of the more honest celebrities, the British comedian Russell Brand, remarked that 'Celebrity in itself is utterly, utterly vacuous: after becoming famous you realize you need nutrition from a higher source.' Here he is acknowledging and recognizing that there is something far greater and more satisfying than fame and wealth. However, in our stubbornness, we do not easily admit that there is more to life than wealth and fame. Instead, our egos can seek out immediate and instant pleasures in the forms of alcohol, drugs, sex, popular music and film, and even gluttony to satisfy our physical desires to fill the void within us, but only temporarily. And so we are beguiled. To avoid the void, we need to ask ourselves what is missing from our lives.

We all live such busy and frantic lives that we tend to become unconscious of the background noise around us and go on 'autopilot'. In our spiritual lives too, there is a low level of awareness of our reality; this is akin to the blindness often used in the glorious Qur'an to describe disbelievers, or those who reject the reality of God and the Hereafter. This state of blindness also hinders us believers from performing our duties attentively. So what can open our eyes to our reality?

At the very crux of a fulfilling life is the central human need for positive relationships with oneself, one's family and one's Creator. This human need for positive relationships is dramatized in Pinocchio, the well-known children's story. Gepetto is an Italian woodcarver who creates Pinocchio the puppet who comes to life. Pinocchio is a jovial character getting up to all sorts of boyish mischief, and the story grips our attention as he has one adventure after another. We identify with the parental care and concern of the 'father' Gepetto, as well as with the waywardness and the unclear direction of the boy. At one point in the story, lost in himself, Pinocchio turns to his 'maker' Gepetto saying, 'Papa, I'm not sure who I am. But if I'm alright with you then I guess I'm alright with me.' This innocent remark embodies a profound truth about relationships: with oneself, with one's Maker and with others. Human beings are social animals depending upon each other for psychological and physical support as well as the spiritual link with their Creator.

Only spiritual intelligence can fill the 'void'

The scenarios posed above rouses the following questions: what is missing from our lives? What can open our eyes to reality? Who is our Creator? The answer lies in spiritual intelligence, the journey to deeper layers of meaning and purpose in life and is a peculiar capability bestowed upon the human being by God that makes him more than just a biological creature dependent on material things. Ralph Waldo Emerson, an American philosopher of the nineteenth century, was a Unitarian or believer in the oneness of God; he cogently summarised spirituality as 'the relationship with God, nature and humanity'. The most comprehensive term used in Islamic literature for the subject of spiritual intelligence is found in Sufism, the science of spiritual excellence and purification (*ihsan* and *tazkiyah*); it explains the inner dimensions of Islamic teachings. One of the first books written on this subject was the letter (*risalah*) of Imam Abul Qasim al-Qushayri (d. 1072). In it, he quotes extensively from various Sufis to explain the subject. For instance, he quotes Muhammad al-Jurayri's definition of Sufism, 'It means taking every sublime moral characteristic and leaving behind every lowly one.' He also said Sufism means maintaining a vigil and awareness over one's states and holding to correct behaviour. For Samnun, it means that 'You possess nothing and nothing possesses you.' For al-Junayd, it means that 'You are solely with God and you have no other attachments.' Ahmad ibn 'Ajibah said, 'It is the knowledge through which one attains Divine nearness, purification of the self and ridding oneself of moral vices and developing moral virtues; it starts with knowledge, continues through constant action and results in obtaining Divine proximity.'

> Sufism is the knowledge and understanding of self-purification and personal and moral development that leads to outward and inward happiness.

The dictionary definition of spirituality

The English word 'spiritual' comes from the Latin *spiritus*, meaning breath. 'Spirituality' means concern with the spirit as opposed to matter, concern with sacred or religious things, the holy and the Divine, concern for a relationship with the soul, and not with external realities. The Qur'an mentions the Divine breath as giving life to the body of Adam, *And I blew my breath into it* (*al-Hijr* 15: 29). In other words, the Divine breath is what gave Adam life and links and connects the human being to his Creator's breath that lives in the heart of man.

Spiritual intelligence is most important

In *The Power of Spiritual Intelligence*, Tony Buzan elegantly explains the purpose of this spiritual intelligence: 'When you are spiritually intelligent you become more aware of the big picture, for yourself and the universe, and your place and purpose in it. Spiritual intelligence is considered by many to be the most important of all our intelligences and has the power to transform your life, civilization, the planet and the course of history.' This inner aspect of human life is not easy to explain in words, and sometimes poetry can be a useful way into understanding and expressing spiritual intelligence. Rumi provides us with a poetic definition:

> O God, show us everything in this house of illusion as it
>   really is,
> No one who has died is sad as a result;
> His grief is that he has not sent enough for the Hereafter,
> He has left the prison behind and finds himself in open
>   fields filled with delight.
> From this place of mourning, the dungeon of pain he has
>   moved to Paradise,

A seat of truth not a palace of falsehood, a precious wine
   not whey.

Here Rumi has effectively paraphrased the blessed Messenger's famous prayer, 'O Lord, show me the truth as it really is, and give me the power to follow it, and show the world to me as it really is, and give me the capacity to avoid it.' (Tirmidhi)

In another place Rumi explains the illusory nature of the material realm: 'If anyone were to tell a baby in the womb: outside is an ordered world, a pleasant earth, wide and open, brimming with thousands of delights and delicious foods – mountains, gardens and fertile fields, its wonders beyond description, why do you stay here drinking blood, in this cramped cell of filth and pain? Unaware of the realty, the baby would turn away in utter disbelief, the blind having no imagination. It has never experienced anything beyond the womb, and cannot visualize such a place.' The reason why the world is called illusory is that it gives the impression of permanence, of being an everlasting destination and that is false, for only the Hereafter (*al-akhirah*) is permanent and everlasting.

> Spiritual intelligence is the knowledge through which one attains Divine nearness, purification of the self and ridding oneself of moral vices and developing strong character; it starts with knowledge, continues through constant action and results in obtaining Divine proximity.

Defining the scope and nature of spiritual intelligence

Spiritual intelligence is the knowledge and understanding of the meaning and purpose of life, and undertaking practices that enhance connection with God and help to acquire the status of God's representative on earth (*khalifah*). For the German philosopher Immanuel Kant, 'Man is dependent on God' and 'needs to believe in a creator in order to function properly'. The Ultimate Reality is God, the Creator and Lord of the universe. The glorious Qur'an intimates that *They only know the outer surface of this present life and are heedless of the life to come. Have they not thought about their own selves? God did not create the heavens and the earth and everything between them without a serious purpose and an appointed time....'* (*al-Rum* 30: 7–8) Therefore, spiritual intelligence is an essentially reflective and active expression of Islamic beliefs of the oneness of God, guidance through the prophets and scripture, and in the life hereafter. That is why spiritual intelligence cannot be regarded as separate from Islam; rather, it is the essence, core and crux of the Islamic way of life.

Spiritual intelligence is about the big questions of life

Spiritual intelligence helps us to understand the human being's relationship with God, the motivation to love and obey Him so that one lives in conformity to the Divine will, or a sense of God-consciousness where one lives in the Divine presence. The Messenger ﷺ alluded to this particular meaning of spiritual intelligence in a tradition known as the Hadith of Gabriel, in which he called spiritual intelligence '*ihsan*', and defined it as 'worshipping God as though you see Him; if you cannot see Him, then remember He sees you' (Bukhari). Islamic teachings provide a clear methodology for developing spiritual intelligence, ways of drawing closer to God, with the purpose of achieving the Lord's pleasure (*ridwan Allah*), Paradise and, eventually, the Beatific Vision in the Hereafter. Spiritual intelligence is *not* about manners or even moral values of compassion, generosity, love or patience; it is about the right kind of consciousness and awareness of the reality around us. It provides answers to the big questions of life, birth, death, suffering, and good and evil; in short, it is concerned with the meaning and the purpose of life.

Spiritual intelligence puts humanity in touch with reality

Spiritual intelligence shows how to express one's relationship with God; the different modes of prayer, singing and reciting litanies,

> Spiritual intelligence is the knowledge and the understanding of reality: it provides insights into the ultimate Reality and helps to distinguish it from the illusions of the material world.

night vigils, fasting and giving charity are ways of growing spiritually. The Prophet of Islam often sought the Lord's help by means of these words: 'O Lord! Help us to remember You, thank You and serve You.' No wonder Telhard de Chardin, the famous Western writer on spiritual intelligence, concludes that 'We are not human beings having a spiritual experience;

we are spiritual beings having a human experience.' You must be spiritual if you are a human being as spiritual intelligence provides the inner strength to cope with life's problems and adversities just as it reveals that the inner is intimately related to the outer, the inner is reflected in the outer, the spiritual world is attached to the physical world. This explains Islam's loathing of monasticism, of detaching oneself from worldly relations; the spiritual cannot be detached from the worldly. Spiritual intelligence is therefore a vital channel allowing Divine grace to act on us and through us to transform the society around us.

Spiritual intelligence develops our resilience to life's problems

People's need to feel connected to God so they can cope with life's vagaries as described in the Qur'anic passage: *Man is created anxious, he is impatient when misfortune befalls him but miserly in good times except those who pray regularly and give their wealth to the poor and needy, who believe in the Day of Judgement, who fear the punishment of their Lord ... who guard their chastity ... that keep their promises, they will be honoured in gardens of bliss.* (*al-Ma'arij* 70: 19–35). The Qur'an teaches us that when you develop spiritual intelligence it allows you to overcome anxiety, fretting about the worries of life, and instead gives energy, vitality and enthusiasm for living. The three signs of misery are anxiety, impatience and miserliness. However, those exempt from these psychological disorders are spiritually intelligent people who have the habit of prayer; they have inner peace and are better able to control the stresses of life. The Qur'an clearly acknowledges the impact of prayer on behaviour by giving it the power to transform human character.

How does spiritual intelligence differ from morals and manners and legal and social rights?

What is the relationship between spiritual intelligence and morals and manners and legal and social rights? It is not a digression to understand the differences between these various subjects and spiritual intelligence as it helps us to focus clearly on our central theme.

Morality is a code of conduct revealed by God and lived by all the Prophets; the final Prophet Muhammad ﷺ explained his purpose as having 'been sent to perfect moral character'. Muslims regard prophetic morality as the overriding guide to individual behaviour which they must adopt in their daily lives. Indeed, it is a universal guide that all rational people can aspire to; a closer look at Islamic morality shows it is a universal code that other religions promote as well. I have explained morality in greater detail in *7 Steps to Moral Intelligence*.

Adab in Arabic means manners or the conventional rules of good behaviour to do with everyday acts such as eating and drinking, dress, meeting and greeting, walking and talking, or speaking and listening. It includes social behaviour, guidance on how to be courteous and polite or pleasant to others so that strong friendly relations can be built among people. One of the most important functions of the Prophet ﷺ was to reform uncivilised and uncouth nomads into a caring and compassionate society.

> Spiritual intelligence is concerned with the connection we have with our Lord, and is the powerhouse that help us to develop our morals (*akhlaq*), manners (*adab*), practice of Islamic ethical-legal rulings (*fiqh*) and fulfil social obligations (*huquq al-'ibad*).

Spiritual intelligence also differs from Islamic ethical-legal rulings (*fiqh*), that specifically deals with the do's (the obligatory, recommended and permitted) and the don'ts (offensive and forbidden). These conventions cover all aspect of a Muslim's life including worship, marriage and divorce, and business. A breach of the law carries penalties either in the worldly life or the Hereafter – but that is not the case with morality. Although a breach of the moral code does not incur any penalty, it carries the significance of troubling the conscience and incurring Divine wrath.

Likewise, spiritual intelligence should not be confused with fulfilling social obligations (*huquq al-'ibad*), such as the rights of parents, relatives, children, neighbours, teachers, friends and even animals. They constitute the desire to meet the needs of others by supporting and respecting them and fulfilling their rights, based on the deeply-held belief that all human beings have common parentage in Adam and Eve. This belief leads to the feelings of brotherhood and sisterhood, the idea that all humans are one family – 'the family of God'. All are equal and should have their human rights protected. Islam expects us to make serving others an important part of our lives.

> The Prophet ﷺ said, 'The best amongst you is the one who benefits others most.' (Tirmidhi)

To sum up, spiritual intelligence is the awareness of the Lord of the universe. It is having faith in His benevolence, trust in His infinite power and accepting the role of being His representative on earth, and being His trusted servant. It is the energy that motivates us to develop strong character and manners and to obey legal and social rules.

The elements of spiritual intelligence

The Qur'an and Sunnah repeatedly describe the disciplines of spiritual intelligence: *taqwa*, meaning God-consciousness, piety, fear of God, awareness and attentiveness; *ikhlas*, meaning sincerity and genuineness in one's intention and actions, and *hubb Allah*, or the love of God. We will explore these later on, but suffice it to say here that the various forms of worship like the five daily prayers (*salawat*), remembrance of God (*dhikr*), the

Divine glorification (*tasbih*), singing spiritual poems (*qasa'id* or *anashid*), invoking His beautiful names (*al-asma' al-husna*), and fasting (*sawm*) are effective spiritual disciplines. The individual is transformed inwardly and draws closer and closer to God, feels happy, recognizes the Lord and lives in His presence. The end game or goal of spiritual intelligence is no less than becoming one of God's friends, who enjoy a state of happiness, bliss and contentment. Spiritual intelligence is the bedrock of a devout, serene and successful life lived for God's sake.

To develop spiritual intelligence you have to be passionate about it. To be successful at something, the fact is that you have to enjoy doing it, believe and engage in it and be passionate about the benefits you will reap at the end. It will be a shame if you simply struggle and strive without being happy, so push yourself forward with joy to take the prize of spiritual intelligence.

KEY POINTS

❀ Happiness does not come from fame or material wealth but from a positive relationship with oneself, one's family and one's Creator.

❀ Spiritual intelligence is the most important form of intelligence because it is applied to the spiritual life and gives us knowledge of life's purpose and enhances our connection with our Creator.

❀ Spiritual intelligence is the foundation upon which we develop our morals, manners, practice of Islamic ethical-legal rulings and fulfilling social obligations.

❀ Spiritual intelligence is built on God-consciousness, sincere motivation and the love of God.

Chapter Two

The Essentials of Spiritual Intelligence: The Prerequisites for *Ihsan*

In this chapter, we shall attempt to explain the essentials of spiritual intelligence in order to gain a deeper understanding of its nature. Spiritual intelligence lies beneath 'the surface' of external practices, daily rituals and noble behaviour, the 'more than you can see' dimension of Islamic teachings. In Chapter 1, it was explained that spiritual intelligence is another name for Sufism or Islamic mysticism, the central, most powerful current of that tidal wave that constitutes the revelation of Islam. For Martin Lings (or Abu Bakr Siraj al-Din), Sufism is both authentic and effectual. This chapter explores the disciplines that underpin spiritual intelligence, training to be obedient and having self-control, achieved through rigorous moral, mental and physical drills. They are our standards and principles that we believe are good to live by as they have been lived by prophets and great people in the past. I have selected following seven spiritual disciplines that are widely recognized by the Sufi masters. Of course, it is not an exhaustive list; however, understanding of these seven key disciplines is a requirement for developing spiritual intelligence (see Diagram 2.1).

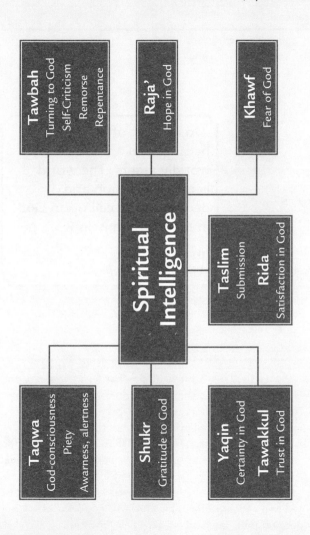

Spiritual Intelligence

Tawbah
Turning to God
Self-Criticism
Remorse
Repentance

Raja'
Hope in God

Khawf
Fear of God

Taslim
Submission
Rida
Satisfaction in God

Taqwa
God-consciousness
Piety
Awareness, alertness

Shukr
Gratitude to God

Yaqin
Certainty in God
Tawakkul
Trust in God

2.1 Seven Disciplines of Spiritual Intelligence

Repentance

Human beings are by nature good; sometimes however we are forgetful and at other times mischievous. We err and sin by ignoring Divine commandments and may even verbally or physically hurt others. Usually, we are remorseful about our misdemeanours, as we feel bad and try to make up for our errors.

This is repentance or *tawbah*, which literally means to turn back from evil to good, from sin to righteousness, from God's displeasure to what pleases Him and from the disobedience of God to obedience to Him. God tells us in

> Do not put off repentance because you are too busy in worldly affairs. The world is only an illusion and deception. So call upon God in tearful submission.
>
> Imam Ghazali,
> *Minhaj al-'Abidin*

the Qur'an: *O believers! Repent before God altogether so that you may prosper* (*al-Nur* 24: 31), and elsewhere *And whoever does an evil or sins and then seeks forgiveness from God, he will find God All-Forgiving and All-Merciful* (*al-Nisa'* 4: 110).

Imam Ghazali observes that repentance is necessary for two reasons. Firstly, the burden of sins hardens the heart and this prevents one from worshipping God and from doing good works. This is the curse of sin as one is deprived of Divine mercy. Therefore, to cleanse oneself from the filth of sin, it is necessary to repent so that one can taste the flavour of faith, worship and good works. To linger in a state of sin can eventually lead to disbelief (*kufr*). Secondly, a sin is Divine disobedience and the sinner has rebelled against his Lord. He therefore owes Him an apology; he is indebted and accountable to his Lord. His good works will not be accepted until he has paid his debt and repented.

What are the conditions of repentance?

Imam Nawawi says that repentance has three conditions: (1) to give up the sin out of Divine fear, (2) to feel ashamed and guilty about doing it, and (3) to resolve not to repeat it again. If the sin was against another person, then there is the fourth condition of requesting pardon and making amends. If we have stolen someone's wealth then it has to be returned. If we have slandered someone then we must seek his forgiveness. Once repentance is complete, then inner transformation begins. A brand new BMW with alloy wheels and a turbo engine replaces an old banger.

How can you give up sins?

In an affluent society, there are ample opportunities to sin, so it is a massive challenge for all of us. So how can we give up sins that are so tempting? Ghazali suggests in *Minhaj al-'Abidin* that we should recall 'the severe punishment of God and the Lord's displeasure. How can you withstand the Hellfire? Will you be able to bear it? You cannot even tolerate the scorching sun, so how will you then be able to put up with the roasting Hellfire? Or being struck by the fiery rods of the angels of hell? Or survive the poisonous venom of Hell's scorpions and snakes? As an intelligent person, how can you carry on sinning and committing crimes? Why do you like to be rebellious and mischievous? Why do you like to be unkind and inhumane to others? If you are mindful and conscious of these truths, then you will soon repent and turn back to the right path. If you have broken away from your Lord by not praying or fasting or simply not carrying out His commandments then start doing these duties immediately and make up for the omissions. If you love some things that are forbidden, then give them up now. If you have been unkind or unfair to someone, then ask for his or her forgiveness. God will raise you in status. As the Prophets taught us "When you seek forgiveness from someone, your status is raised."'

Abu Hurayrah relates that the Prophet ﷺ used to seek God's forgiveness and turn to Him in repentance more than seventy times each day! (Bukhari) Anas ibn Malik reports that he once described God's pleasure at someone's repentance as follows: 'God is more pleased with the repentance of His slave than anyone of you is pleased with finding his camel that he had lost in the desert.' (Bukhari) In brief, real repentance results in a pure heart that confesses its sins as soon as they are discovered and resolves to give them up for the sake of God. The first outcome is a clear conscience as one has sought God's forgiveness and from those people whom you may have offended, and the second is that it builds our relationship with God.

> The Prophet ﷺ said: 'God Almighty extends His hand of forgiveness at night to forgive those who committed evil during the day and He extends His hand during the day to forgive those who committed evil during the night. He will do this until the sun rises from the west.' (Muslim)

Taqwa: The sense of God-consciousness

The second discipline of spiritual intelligence is *taqwa*, an Arabic noun that is derived from the verb *ittaqa* which means 'to be aware, be on one's guard, to protect oneself'. The verb *ittaqa* with its various permutations occurs nearly seventy times, and its imperative form *ittaqu* ('fear God') appears frequently in the Qur'an. We are being warned us to protect ourselves from things that will cause us harm, which includes all sins and criminal activities. The idea one gets from these different meanings of *taqwa* is that the believer is expected to be constantly on his guard, lest he fall into the temptations of the self and of Satan. It expresses a state of alertness, awareness and attentiveness, and a meticulous sense of duty to the Lord. This leads to the idea of 'fear of God', a common working translation of *taqwa*, but the English word 'piety' is more accurate. Therefore, one who has *taqwa* is pious, as the pious one fears to displease his Lord, Master and Creator.

Scholars define taqwa

Ibrahim bin Adham says '*Taqwa* is that people do not find a fault in your speech, and the angels do not find a fault in your action, whilst the angel of the throne sees no fault in your inner motives.' Waqadi defines *taqwa* as 'decorating your inner self for the Lord as you would dress up smartly for people'. 'Abdullah ibn 'Umar was once asked to explain the meaning of *taqwa* and he replied, 'When you walk a narrow steep path hemmed in by thorny bushes and lots of potholes, you tread very carefully so that your clothes don't get entangled by thorns and you're not hurt.' This is an apt simile for illustrating the meaning of *taqwa*: the journey of life is a narrow, steep and rough path hemmed on one side by selfish desires and on the other by Satan, so one has to exercise extreme caution and awareness to avoid falling into the traps of Satan or becoming overwhelmed by life's tests. The scholars also define *taqwa* as ridding one's self of evil traits and embellishing it with good ones.

The fruits of taqwa

A pious person (*muttaqi*) is spiritually awake and alert, enlightened and attached to his Lord, who is promised prosperity here and in the Hereafter. The Qur'an promises them help and support: *Know that God is with the pious (al-Tawbah* 9: 36). This means God will be enough for them. As the All-Hearing and All-Knowing, He guarantees the pious support for success and good fortune through His grace, so they have comfort of knowing that God's mercy is with them. The pious also receive knowledge and wisdom from their Lord.

A reward associated with *taqwa* is receipt of the criterion *al-furqan*; Imam Razi explains that it can be given either in the worldly life or the Hereafter. In the world, it can be either the inward state of one's heart or outward actions, and to those whom it has been given will be blessed with guidance and realization of truth. In the Hereafter, those who receive it will have forgiveness and Paradise. Another reward of *taqwa* is abundant sustenance, as a constant fear that haunts people is how their needs will be fulfilled. God promises the pious that He shall provide for them from where they least expect it*: And whoever fears God, He shall make a way out for him and We will provide him from where he has no expectation (al-Talaq* 65: 2). In other words He shall deliver him from the doubts of the world and punishment in the Hereafter.

Tawakkul: Trust and reliance in God

In English, trust means having a firm belief in the reliability of a person who is truthful, a confident expectation, a person or thing confided in. Imam Ghazali remarks that *tawakkul* has three meanings: firstly, accepting predestination, being satisfied with Divine providence and believing that whatever God has planned for one cannot be changed. God says *And in God let the believers put their trust (Ibrahim* 14: 11). Secondly, it means to rely on God's help and support at all times, He will help him and give him strength. Thirdly, it refers to putting trust in God to provide for one's livelihood, provisions and daily needs. God says *And whoever trusts God He is sufficient for him* (*al-Talaq* 65: 3) and *Once you have taken a decision then put your trust in God* (*Al 'Imran* 3: 159).

Tawwakul is trusting God with regards to one's affairs, which includes livelihood, health and well-being as well as honour and dignity, such that whatever happens one knows that it is God's will and therefore will not complain about it. One becomes convinced that one's vital needs are in the control of one's Lord and Creator and no one else can interfere with this nor can anyone else help besides Him. When one has such trust and confidence in one's heart and reliance on God and looks to no one else, then one is a *mutawakkil* or one who truly trusts in God.

The one who puts trust in God is like a bird

We seem to depend on the material things that we possess, our careers, houses, cars, gadgets, wealth, reputation, family and friends and therefore our dependence on God seems to lessen as our dependence on these things increases. Perhaps this is why the Shariah has discouraged us from being materialistic by forbidding us to hoard things, to take interest, and instead encourages us to give interest-free loans to others, to give away any surplus that we may have and be generous. 'Umar reports that the Messenger ﷺ discouraged us from being money-orientated and said: 'If you all depend on God with due reliance, He will certainly provide for you as He does for the birds who leave their nests hungry in the morning and return with full bellies at dusk.' (Tirmidhi) There is a similar report from Abu Hurayrah that the Prophet ﷺ said: 'A group of men and women whose hearts were like those of birds shall enter Paradise.' (Muslim) The trust that Abraham ﷺ had in his Lord was proverbial, it is said that when he was about to be thrown into Nimrod's fire the Angel Gabriel offered to save him. Abraham ﷺ declined saying 'My Lord is fully aware of my circumstances.' Ibn 'Abbas relates that when Abraham ﷺ was thrown into the fire, he said: 'God alone is sufficient for us, and He is the Best Disposer of affairs.' Putting trust in God is a powerful way to free one's mind of worldly needs and worries, as well as showing one's profound belief in the Divine providence. It is therefore an important pillar of spiritual intelligence as it reflects deep faith, a sense of dependency and trust in God.

Khawf: The fear of God

The third important discipline of spiritual intelligence is closely related to piety. Fear is an unpleasant emotion caused by exposure to danger, or an expectation of future danger. It is a spiritual discipline characterized by being alarmed and horrified, being full of anxiety as result of disobeying God in the past, and dreading His severe punishment now and in the hereafter. The dread is realizing one's defencelessness, inadequacy and weakness in the face of God's immense power. Fear is not a negative emotion as it has a benefit: it motivates us to obey God and follow the Shariah. God Most Exalted says: *I am the only One Who you should fear* (al-Baqarah 2: 40) and *[O Prophet], your Lord's punishment is truly severe* (al-Buruj 85: 12). This means one should obey God, remember and give thanks to Him, and not forget Him nor be unthankful. The Qur'an frequently evokes fear of God as it is a motivator and a deterrent. The motivation is attaining Paradise: *Those who fear the time when they will stand before their Lord, for them will be two gardens* (al-Rahman 55: 46). Ahmad Zaruq remarks that 'Fear of God motivates one to act and it means that one has regard for the majesty and splendour of God and fears that God will take revenge.'

The Messenger describes the ordeal of Hell

The Messenger ﷺ emphasized in various ways the need to fear God, mentioning Hell's torments and the terrors of Judgement Day. He ﷺ said, 'On Judgement Day, Hell will be brought forward and it will be like a giant cooking pot with 70,000 cables attached to it and each cable will be pulled by 70,000 angels.' (Muslim) Hell is described as a fearsome gigantic cauldron that is held in place by 4.9 billion angels; we can picture it as a planet larger than the Earth, striking terror in our hearts and warning us that there will be no shortage of space! Abu Hurayrah relates that: 'We were in the company of the Messenger of God ﷺ when we heard a loud bang. Thereupon the Messenger of God ﷺ said, "Do you know what that is?" We said, "God and His Messenger know better." He said, "That is a stone which was thrown into Hell seventy years ago and it has finally reached the bottom."' (Muslim) Developing this fear of God was one of the prime functions of the Prophet ﷺ who is referred to in the Qur'an as the warner (*nazir*). Nu'man ibn Bashir reports the Messenger of God ﷺ as saying, 'On Judgement Day, the least tortured person in Hell will have burning coal placed under his feet and as a result his brain will boil. Yet he will think that he has been tortured the most.' (Bukhari)

The Messenger motivates:
Do anything to save yourselves from Hell

Wisdom is essential for the development of spiritual intelligence; the pinnacle of wisdom lies in the fear of God. Anas ibn Malik reports that the Messenger of God ﷺ once delivered a sermon the like of which he had never heard before. He said, 'If you knew what I know, you would laugh little and cry more.' Upon hearing this, those present covered their faces and began sobbing.

(Bukhari) 'Adiyy ibn Hatim relates that the Messenger of God ﷺ said, 'Everyone will speak to his Lord without a mediator between them. He shall look to his right side and will see only the good deeds he has done, he shall look to his left and will see only the evil deeds he had done, and he shall look in front of him and will see nothing but the Fire before his eyes. So protect yourselves from the Fire, even if it is just giving half a date (in charity).' (Tirmidhi) The Prophet's purpose in inculcating a fear of God in his Companions was to make them more conscientious and responsible.

Raja': Be ever hopeful of God's kindness

The Arabic verb *raja* means 'to hope', which is the combination of expectation and desire for a certain thing; in other words, an expectation for a positive and desirable outcome that would be satisfying. Feelings of hope reduce the burden of apprehension and ignorance. Imam Ghazali defines hope as 'having joy at the realization of God's grace and mercy and the expectation that he will be blessed with it'. God Most Exalted wants us to be ever hopeful of His mercy and care: *Say, My servants who have harmed yourselves by their own excess, do not despair of God's mercy. God forgives all sins: He is truly the most Forgiving, the most Merciful* (al-Zumar 39: 53) and *My mercy encompasses all things* (al-A'raf 7: 156).

The Messenger ﷺ was always full of hope: he had a positive attitude to life and as this is a contagious emotion so too were his Companions ever hopeful. 'Ubadah ibn al-Samit narrates that the Messenger of God ﷺ said: 'The one who bears witness that there is no true god except God, He is alone and has no partner, and that Muhammad is His servant and messenger, that Jesus is His servant and messenger, and His Word that He communicated to Mary and His spirit which He sent to her, and that Paradise is true and Hell is true, then God will take him into Paradise no matter what deeds he did.' (Muslim)

The feeling of hope is a spiritual discipline based on one of the four beliefs: (1) that God has been very generous and kind to one in the past; (2) God has promised giving immense rewards for the good that one does; (3) God has blessed me beyond my capabilities; and (4) His mercy is vast and overwhelms His anger and wrath.

> Abu Hurayrah relates that he heard the Messenger of God ﷺ saying: 'After God had created all creatures, He wrote on top of the Throne, "My mercy overcomes My anger."' (Bukhari)

Can a woman burn her child?

The Messenger ﷺ developed in his Companions this amazing quality of continual hopefulness. 'Umar ibn al-Khattab relates that some prisoners were brought before the Messenger of God ﷺ, and amongst them was a woman who was anxiously looking for something. When she saw a child among the prisoners, she rushed to the child and grabbed it, pressed it against her breasts and gave it milk. Seeing this motherly care the Messenger of God ﷺ said, 'Do you think this woman would ever burn her child?' We said, 'By God, she would never do that.' He told them: 'God is more kind to his people than this woman is to her child.' (Muslim) Abu Hurayrah relates that the Messenger of God ﷺ said, 'God divided His kindness into one hundred parts. He kept ninety-nine parts, and sent down only one part to earth. It is through this one part that creatures deal compassionately with one another, so much so that an animal lifts its hoof over its young lest it should hurt it.' (Bukhari)

Taslim and rida: Complete submission to and satisfaction in God

Spiritual intelligence is one's attachment, awareness and attentiveness to God and this is symbolized in submission and satisfaction with Him so much so that the spiritually intelligent declares boldly that 'I am happy with God as my Lord, with Muhammad as my master and prophet, and Islam as way of life.' Happiness and satisfaction are mutual and reciprocal feelings, which is why the Qur'an proclaims that *God is satisfied with them and they are satisfied with him* (al-Bayyinah 98: 8). Being satisfied means being content, happy and fulfilled with what comes from the Divine, such as the difficulties and hardships

> Hope and fear need to be balanced like the two wings of a bird. When they are equal, the bird is balanced and its flight is perfect. However, when one of them is lacking, the bird lose its ability to fly. When both wings are missing, the bird falls to its death.
>
> Al-Qushayri

of life, the trials and tribulations of the world, the physical and emotional pain and suffering. This is complete satisfaction with God, the One Who controls all human affairs.

The Arabic noun *rida* is translated as being satisfied or well pleased with something. The Sufis understand it as being satisfied in the face of hardships and difficulties; in other words, to welcome and receive hardships with a cheerful smile, being satisfied whether one receives or not, and never being annoyed with the Divine decree. God is satisfied with His servant when he is satisfied with all that comes from the Lord: this is mutual satisfaction.

The sages of the past have provided us with great wisdom on satisfaction, so relish these gems. Abu al-Daqqaq said 'Satisfaction is not that you never experience trials; satisfaction is that you do not object to the Divine decree and judgement.' He explained this when one of his young disciples asked: 'Does a person know if God is pleased with him?' The master's answer was no, for how could he know that when His pleasure is hidden. However, the young man insisted 'but He does know that!' The master asked how. He replied: 'When my heart is pleased with God I feel that He is pleased with me too,' upon which Abu al-Daqqaq said, 'Young man, you have spoken well!'

Rabi'ah al-'Adwiyyah, the famous saint of Basra, was asked 'When is the servant satisfied?' She replied, 'When hardships delight him as much as blessings.' She was on a mission, for such was her passion that she wanted humanity to love God first then Paradise, to put the Absolute before the relative. One day someone saw her walking hurriedly with a blazing torch in one hand and a bucket of water in the other and asked her, 'O Rabi'ah! What is this?' She responded, 'I am going to burn God's Paradise with fire and extinguish the fire of Hell with water so that people no longer worship God for Paradise or for being saved from the fire of Hell. Instead, they should be satisfied with Him.'

The excellence of submission and satisfaction

Satisfaction is far higher than patience as it is complete submission to the Divine will and decree; the traveller on the Divine path considers difficulties and hardship as mercy. When the Companion Bilal was on his deathbed he said with a smile, 'For me, this is a moment of real happiness, as I will now meet my beloved and his Companions.'

The blessed Messenger ﷺ said, 'When you avoid forbidden actions, you shall become the best worshiper, when you are satisfied with God's decree, you shall become the richest, when you are good to your neighbour, you shall become a true believer, and when you like for other people what you like for yourself you shall become a true Muslim. Do not laugh excessively as too much laughter deadens the heart.' (Tirmidhi) A story about the Companion 'Urwah ibn Zubayr illustrates this satisfaction with Divine decree. After enduring a long illness, his leg had to be amputated on the night that one of his sons died. When people came to pay their condolences, he would say 'O Lord, all praise is for You! You blessed me with seven children and now You have taken one and I have six left; I had four limbs and now You have taken one and I am left with three. If today You have taken from me, yesterday You gave it to me in the first place; if You have tested me, then You have also given me comfort.' The reward for this great quality of satisfaction is no less than Paradise, for *God has promised the believers, both men and women, gardens graced with flowing streams where they will remain; good, peaceful homes of lasting bliss; and – greatest of all – God's satisfaction* (al-Tawbah 9: 72).

Shukr: Gratitude and appreciating and thanking others

The seeker of spiritual intelligence is eager to learn and develop disciplines that bring him closer to God, among these is gratitude, which is to be thankful, appreciative of others and acknowledging them openly and desiring to return the favour to them in a better way. Praising the goodness of others is a common way of showing gratitude as is thanking people (*shukr*). God is al-Shakur, the Most Appreciative, Who expresses thankfulness through bounteous reward. He acknowledges the tiniest good deeds of humanity and greatly rewards them. His appreciation of good acts takes many forms by praising righteous people, giving them favours and rewards, and removing difficulties from their lives. The 'thankful' nature of God is clearly illustrated in a story told by the Messenger who said, 'A traveller was passing through an oasis and came to a well, and he climbed down it and drank to his heart's content. When he came out of the well, he saw a thirsty dog licking the wet sand around the side of the well. The man went down again and filled his moccasin with water and gave the dog the water to drink. God thanked the man.' (Bukhari) Notice here that God is thanking the traveller who gave water to the thirsty dog, not the other way around. God rewards our small deeds many times over, sometimes ten times, sometimes several hundred and at other times 'without bounds and limits'. This is the thankful Lord. The Qur'an proclaims: *If you are thankful I will increase you and if you are ungrateful, then My punishment is severe* (*Ibrahim* 14 : 7).

Hasan ibn Thabit was a renowned poet in the Prophet's day. When he became Muslim, he praised the Messenger ﷺ with his eloquent tongue, and one day he composed the following beautiful eulogy:

> My eyes have not seen anyone more beautiful then you
> No woman ever gave birth to one like you,
> You were formed without blemish,
> Were made as you wished to be created.

The Messenger ﷺ was so moved by this eulogy that he gave the poet his cloak and asked him to sit on the pulpit. This is gratitude: receiving praise from others with thanks, and is an example of selfless action and acknowledgment of the kindness offered. The Messenger ﷺ once said of Abu Bakr's service: 'There is no one whose favour I have not repaid except for Abu Bakr's. God will reward him on the Day of Judgement. No one's wealth has benefited me more than that of Abu Bakr's. If I were to choose a friend, it would be Abu Bakr. Beware, for your master is God's friend.' (Bukhari) It is greatness of mind

Essentials

that acknowledges every good deed. The Messenger was very appreciative of his Companions' efforts and would praise them at every opportunity. Once he said to Abu Bakr, 'You were my Companion in the cave and you will again be my Companion at the Fountain of Paradise.' (Bukhari) To show the Messenger's acknowledgement of the great work of his Companions, the Prophet ﷺ conferred rich titles upon them. For example, he called Abu Bakr 'the truthful' (al-Siddiq), 'Umar, 'the criterion of truth' (al-Faruq), 'Uthman, 'the benevolent' (al-Ghaniyy), 'Ali, 'the gate of knowledge' (Bab al-'Ilm), Ibn 'Abbas, 'scholar of the faithful community' (Hibr al-Ummah), and Khalid ibn Walid, 'the sword of God' (Sayf Allah).

However, there are reports in which the Messenger 'disliked praising others in front of them'. Imam Nawawi in *Riyad al-Salihin* tries to reconcile these reports as follows: 'If the one who is praised has strong faith, is well disciplined and has sound judgment and there is no fear of spoiling him with praise, in that case there is no harm lavishing praise on someone. However, if there is a danger that praise will make him feel self-righteous then don't praise him.' So be thankful to those who were good to you, praise them, give them gifts, and remember what the Prophet ﷺ said 'Whoever is not thankful to people is not thankful to God.' Imam Ghazali regards this discipline as the most significant pillar of spiritual intelligence.

KEY POINTS

❀ Spiritual intelligence is built on seven essentials.

❀ These essentials are God-consciousness, gratitude to God, certainty and trust in God, submission to and satisfaction in God, fear of God, hope in God and repentance to God.

Chapter Three

The Spiritual Intelligence of the Beloved Messenger

In order to understand an intellectual concept clearly, the preferred method is to look at a role model, a living example, and to see a practical demonstration of it. This chapter provides a living, walking and talking role model of a spiritually intelligent person. Here you will read about the Prophet of Islam: his prayers, night vigils, fasting, seclusion, supplications, and yearnings for the Divine. We will catch glimpses of his commitment to God, a heart devoted to God that exudes inner light and beauty as it is immersed in the Divine love. The Prophet's spiritual intelligence was demonstrated through his relationships with his Companions, being selfless with them, giving time to them, affirming their faith and works, trusting them and, above all, caring for them. This is perhaps why the term 'heirs of the prophets' (*warathat al-anbiya'*) is used for those scholars who practise the Prophet's teachings fully, who walk in his footsteps and follow his noble example. The Qur'an points to a striking feature of this particular community as conscious of the Hereafter as they are 'direction-conscious' and 'path-minded' people.

Spiritual intelligence is expressed variously: firstly, through practising moral virtues of kindness, humility, gentleness, generosity and forgiveness; and secondly, through keeping away oneself from vices such as anger, greed, jealousy and arrogance.

A purpose of spiritual intelligence is to cure these sicknesses. These restraints include fasting, observing the night vigil, controlling one's speech, limiting interaction with people, Divine remembrance, deep reflection, eating halal and avoiding forbidden things. Each one of these seven restraints that are in fact

> *There is a beautiful role model in the Messenger of God for those of you who who have set their hopes on God and the Hereafter and always remember God abundantly.*
> (*al-Ahzab* 33: 21)

remedies was practised, lived and prescribed by the blessed Messenger ☀; they represent certain aspects of his wonderful life. Such a sublime and careful way of living can be called a reflective life with lifelong learning, a just life, and a holistic life.

The Messenger ☀ possessed a perfect intellect: he was adept and skilled at reasoning, and full of the knowledge given to him by the All-Knowing Lord, with a clear understanding of the world around him, and the mental powers of the cleverest person in his society. The truth of this statement can often be seen clearly in all of his beautiful teachings, which are full of wisdom. He is always teaching how to be good to others, how to get closer to the Lord of the universe by being obedient and grateful to Him, and by appreciating the bounties that He has given us. The Prophet's intelligence was expressed through his moral character and the values he taught, shown by his moral character, his polite and courteous manners and, of course, his spiritual devotions day and night. In this chapter, we are going to read about the Prophet's spiritual exercises, dedication and longings for the Divine as they will encourage others to follow him. One final point about his intellect is the influence of his wise words. He spoke with warm sincerity that affected his tone of voice and the eloquent and inspiring fluency of his words that penetrated deep into the souls of his listeners. When he spoke to them about Paradise he brought to them a vision of its gorgeous gardens, graced with flowing streams. When he described the Divine light they could literally see it beaming down from Heaven. The many volumes of Hadith literature testify to the wonderfully precise and pithy eloquence of his Arabic that was comprehensive in its meanings (*jawami' al-kalam*).

The Prophet's simple life

The blessed Messenger ﷺ practised scrupulous self-discipline and abstained from many ordinary pleasures, for the purpose of pleasing his Lord and enhancing his spirituality. He adopted an ascetic lifestyle of poverty; his poverty was the matter of choice not necessity for him as there was plenty of wealth available to him from various sources. He did not like to hoard money and led a life of simplicity, sleeping on straw mats that left noticeable marks on his body and clothes. This would upset his Companions, and once someone offered him a soft mat to sleep on. His response was: 'What have I to do with this world? My place in this world is like that of a traveller who is walking through the desert on a hot day, he takes a nap under a tree and then leaves it behind him.' (Abu Ya'la)

This was the Prophet's mind-set and attitude towards worldly comforts. He neither forbade them to his Companions nor encouraged or promoted a life of luxury. According to one narration, when God Almighty offered him gold that would fill the Valley of Makkah, he replied, 'Lord! I would prefer to be hungry one day and eat the next. The day I eat, I will praise You and give thanks to You; when I remain hungry, I will seek Your help and call upon You.' (Tirmidhi) His wife 'A'ishah tells us that 'The Messenger of God ﷺ never had a meal large enough to last until supper, nor a supper large enough to last until the next meal; and he never had two of anything: not two shirts, two cloaks, two loincloths, nor two pairs of shoes.' He would rarely eat twice a day. Such was his sense of reliance on the Lord that he wanted to remain aloof from worldly things; he was happy with a small amount of worldly sustenance. He once prayed 'O God! Make the provision of Muhammad's family such that it meets their bare needs.' (Muslim)

One day the Prophet's daughter Fatimah brought him a freshly-baked loaf of bread. It smelt delicious and she proudly said to him, 'O father, I baked this myself and brought to you because I did not feel at ease eating it without sharing it with you.' The blessed Messenger ﷺ replied, 'I haven't eaten anything for three days, so this will be the first morsel.' (Bayhaqi) The Prophet ﷺ ate little because he knew the dangers of filling the stomach, 'When you are full,' he would say, 'the Devil runs within your veins, so make his path difficult by remaining hungry.' He also said, 'The son of Adam fills no vessel worse than his stomach.' Many spiritual masters regard gluttony and overeating as dangerous habits that not only ruin physical health but also spiritual health. A lack of food means less energy and, as a consequence, a person will drink less, sleep little and speak less. In a way, this provides a necessary distance from people, which enables one to devote more time to spiritual matters.

These matters are covered in detail in al-Shabrawi's *The Degrees of the Soul*, who provides invaluable insights on this subject. He writes, 'Jihad is an obligation, and the essence of it is to forsake all habits.... In particular, these six: to eat, sleep and talk less; isolate oneself from people; to make Remembrance constantly and to reflect effectively. Moderation is required in each of these things and they have said that all the other things are only to be diminished not abandoned altogether. The effective thing in this part is to eat only when hungry, and then to less than satiety. The Prophet, may God's blessing be upon him, omitted supper when he had eaten lunch and omitted lunch when he had eaten supper.'

The blessed Messenger ﷺ was sent as a guide and he communicated the Divine message eloquently and effectively to his people. The reasons being that one can easily fall into speaking ill of others. In fact, we commit more sins with the tongue than with any other limb, slandering others, insulting others, using obscene language or cursing, arguing with people, revealing the secrets of others, mocking and jeering at others, and even lying, backbiting, slandering, and being pretentious. The Prophet ﷺ said that, 'When I was shown Hell, I saw people were tearing their faces with their nails. I asked Gabriel ﷺ, "Who are they?" And he replied, "Those who backbite and slander people."' (Bukhari)

The Prophet's days and nights spent in worship

The Prophet's worship consisted of the five daily prayers, the night vigil (*tahajjud*), recitation of the glorious Qur'an, remembrance (*dhikr*) and fasting. He fasted sometimes day after day, a form of fasting unique to him, where he would not eat at sunset and continue into the next day and the day after. This will go on for several days without a break. People would remark that it looked as if he would not stop fasting, but then sometimes he would not fast for so long that people would say he would never fast. When some Companions tried to imitate his practice of continuous fasting, they became so weak after a day that they could not

33

stand up for prayer. The Prophet ﷺ asked them what they were doing. When they told him that they were fasting day after day and following his Sunnah, he told them, 'I spend nights with my Lord, and He gives me to eat and drink. Who amongst you is like me?' (Muslim) His favourite practice was to fast every Monday and Thursday, explaining that 'There are the days when deeds are presented, so I love to make it so that, when my deeds are presented, I am fasting.' (Tirmidhi) He liked to fast on Monday in order to honour the blessed day of his birth. He often fasted the three days of whiteness, which are the fourteen, fifteen and sixteenth days of each lunar month. This meant that he would fast between nine and eleven days every month.

After the pre-dawn prayer (Fajr), the Prophet ﷺ would sit cross-legged on his prayer mat remembering God by His beautiful names (*asma' al-husna*) until sunrise. He would then offer four or six prayer-cycles (*rak'at*) called Ishraq. He praised the excellence of this prayer and advised that praying in praying it regularly one's sins are forgiven even if they are as much as the foam on the surface of the sea. At mid-morning, he would perform the Duha prayer. He had a remarkable attachment to prayer that he would fondly ask Bilal: 'Stand up, Bilal, and give me peace of mind with the prayer.' After the sunset prayer he would offer between four and twelve prayer-cycles of Awwabin, such was his love for the prayer. This means that the Prophet ﷺ formally prayed nine times daily: the five obligatory daily prayers and four supererogatory prayers, the total time of which would have been more than two hours. He would often pray silently by raising his hands up to his shoulders, with his palms facing the sky, calling upon his Lord; his prayers and supplications will be looked at in Chapter 4.

> The Prophet ﷺ said, 'I am most delighted when I pray.' (Ahmad)

Lifelong learning and teaching

Of course the Prophet ﷺ was Divinely educated: *He taught you what you knew not* (al-Nisa' 4: 113) and *It is the Lord of mercy who taught the Qur'an. He created man and taught him to communicate* (al-Rahman 55: 1–4). 'Man' here refers to the blessed Prophet ﷺ; therefore, for him, it was a matter of lifelong teaching rather than lifelong learning, as he was Divinely taught by the Almighty. Lifelong learning is something we all should be engaged in for our constant mental and spiritual development. It is useful for us to reflect on the Prophet's method of teaching in educating the Companions.

The Prophet ﷺ was highly motivated to teach the glorious Qur'an. Once he had received a revelation and memorized it himself, he would summon one of several scribes to come and preserve it for posterity. He would encourage other Companions to memorize the new passage. In this way, many of the Companions memorized the entire Qur'an, and he was passionate that children should learn it. When delegations from Arab tribes came to Madinah to embrace Islam, the Prophet ﷺ would dispatch a learned Companion with them to teach them the *adhan*, the prayer and the Qur'an. He also encouraged parents to teach children and to motivate them. He gave them glad tidings of the most exquisite spiritual rewards in the Hereafter. For example, he

> The Prophet ﷺ said: 'The best amongst you is the one who learns and teaches the Qur'an.' (Bukhari)

said 'Every father who teaches his child the Qur'an in this world will be crowned in Paradise on the Day of Resurrection. By this crown, the people of Paradise will know him as one who taught his children the Qur'an.' (Tabarani) The reading of the glorious Qur'an is an important spiritual activity as well as being an educational exercise. This is why it is very prevalent and is widely used as a means of spiritual progress.

On another occasion the blessed Prophet ﷺ said, 'Recite the Qur'an as it will intercede for its reader on the Day of Judgement.' (Muslim) Ibn 'Abbas relates that the beloved Messenger said, 'A person without the Qur'an in his heart is like a wrecked house.' (Tirmidhi)

The Prophet's balanced life

The distinguishing characteristic of a wise and spiritually intelligent person is a balanced lifestyle, which has the right amount of work and family time, and the correct ratio of time spent in earning a livelihood and socializing. The blessed Messenger ﷺ was just that person with a balanced life in equilibrium. As we read the accounts of his time at home with his family, we see that perfect balance between his role as a prophet of God, a spiritual guide, a leader and a teacher. The Prophet ﷺ took great care of his family by spending time with them and doing all kinds of domestic chores, such as repairing or cleaning his clothes, mending his shoes, milking the goats, fetching water for ablutions, and other household chores. He was effectively at the service of his family, helping them with their tasks, listening to their jokes, and laughing with them. On one occasion, the Prophet ﷺ challenged his wonderful wife 'A'ishah to race with him; he was in his fifties and she was in her late teens. She won the race. Some months later, he challenged her again to another race, but this time he beat her. 'A'ishah said that he had won because she had grown fat and plump and he began to laugh, saying, 'This pays you back for that.' (Ibn Majah) It is little wonder why he would say that 'The best of you are those who are best to their families, and I am the best to my family.' (Tirmidhi)

The Prophet ﷺ felt very comfortable doing jobs that other leaders might consider mean and beneath their status; by doing so, he was being humble and also teaching his followers an important lesson in humility. This is the virtue where one forsakes the glory of one's social status and pride and assumes a lower position than one's equals. Perhaps more accurately, humility means that a person sees himself as having no special value or distinctive worth and does not consider himself to be

> *Tell them Prophet, if you love God then follow me so that God may love you and forgive your sins. (Al 'Imran 3: 31)*

above others. The following story is a beautiful example of his humility. When they had set up camp during an expedition, the Prophet ﷺ instructed his Companions to roast the sheep that had been slaughtered. He assigned each person a task: one man to skin it, another to prepare it for cooking and for himself he said, 'I will go and fetch the firewood.' The Companions said, 'O Messenger of God! Let us take care of everything.' He replied, 'I know that you will do it well, but I hate to be different from the rest of you and God dislikes a person who sees himself as better than his friends.' (Ibn Majah) He knew well that pretending to be great and above others and wanting others accept you as their leader were worldly things that were disdainful in his view. God has presented us with a perfect example of a spiritually intelligent man who loved Him dearly, who cared for others and who is 'the way' to the Divine.

Conclusion

The purpose of spiritual life is to get a deeper understanding of God, inner knowledge, peace of mind, a process to renew the heart, as one begins to live with God. The various spiritual disciplines and exercises, the simple life, lifelong learning and the balanced life of the Messenger ﷺ is the model for us to imitate, to follow him in his longing and thirst for God.

KEY POINTS

- ﷺ The Prophet is our foremost example of a spiritually intelligent person.

- ﷺ He lived simply, avoiding excess and materialism.

- ﷺ He spent his days and nights in worship; part of his spiritual routine was special to him as a prophet, and the rest was an example to humanity.

- ﷺ He lived a life of perfect balance between his role as Prophet, teacher and leader, worship of his Lord, and time spent with his family.

Chapter Four

The Seven Steps of Spiritual Intelligence

In the 1970s, when my spiritual guide and teacher Pir Muhammad Karam Shah was imprisoned for standing up against the tyranny of Pakistan's government, he asked his son to bring his books to his prison cell. Why? He wanted to keep learning and growing, even in a dark and dingy prison cell. He knew well that if you stop growing, then you are on a slippery slope downhill. Every year the tree blossoms and bears fruit but it also grows a little, and becomes taller and sturdier. So every year you must grow a little like the tree. To produce the sugar that it needs to grow, a tree depends on nutrients that it absorbs from the soil, the carbon dioxide it transpires from the air, and the energy provided by the sun. Similarly, the traveller on this path requires ingredients too. Chapters 1 and 2 define the meaning and scope required for growth, as well as its disciplines, while Chapter 3 describes how the beloved Messenger ﷺ put these disciplines into practice and lived a life filled with devotion. This chapter explores how we can become spiritually intelligent one step at a time.

How much do we remember?	%
What we are told	10
What we see	20
What we both see and hear	50
What we say	80
What we both say and do	90

4.1 How we learn

Research about learning shows that the more actively involved we are, the more we retain (see Diagram 4.1). This is summed up in the saying: 'Tell me, I forget. Show me, I remember. Involve me, I understand.' Therefore, the best way to develop spiritual intelligence is to read and then inwardly digest what you have read; in other words, reflect and think about what you have read, and then follow it with repetition. Then if you can share what you have learnt with someone else, then you are likely to remember 80% of this book's content.

Adults are responsible for their own growth, and this requires change, hard work and willingness to develop new skills, learn new subjects and make new connections. Yet change is often uncomfortable and this is one of the reasons why so few of us carry on growing. Change requires us to move into unfamiliar

Surely God does not change a people until they change themselves. (al-Ra'd 13: 11)

territory where we may feel unsafe. Taking a new step may seem risky, even frightening, but this is what change is about. This is what leads to growth, as without growth we are destined to

40

remain stunted like immovable objects and stuck in a rut.

Another barrier to spiritual growth is being too busy, the other name for worldliness, love of the world, trapped in the consumer society's agenda of producing and consuming more and more to the detriment of fulfilling our religious obligations. A key ingredient to succeeding is giving quality time, not leftover time, when we are exhausted after a hard day's work. It is the quality time spent in worship and the remembrance of God that brings about spiritual growth. Avoid being B.U.S.Y., as this stands for Being Under Satan's Yoke!

The Prophet ﷺ said that God said, 'I declare war on anyone who has enmity against My friend. My servant draws near to Me by carrying out obligatory duties and then continues to draw nearer through voluntary acts until I love him. And when I love him I become his ear by which he hears, his eyes by which he sees, his hands by which he grasps and his feet by which he walks. If he asks, I will give him, and if he seeks protection, I will protect him.' (Bukhari) Spirituality is about becoming a person in the fullest sense – becoming a deputy of God (*khalifat Allah*), who fulfils the covenant (*mithaq*) that human beings made with God in their disembodied state in the world of souls (*'alam al-arwah*) before they enter this world, the place where we are all tested. Spirituality is freedom from the clutches of physical existence and dependency on the material world and its trappings; it is this newfound freedom to become self-conscious that gives us the amazing spiritual power to show love and altruism. Self-consciousness makes us more aware of the Divine and gives us a deeper understanding of reality. This sharply-focused awareness of God leads to realization and recognition of the Creator. The obvious and natural response is submission to the Divine will, the desire to worship Him, and to turn to Him in repentance and gratitude. This gradually leads to detachment from love of the world, and a transformation of the whole person takes place that leads to an enriched way of living. This is real change brought about by new and deep thinking: it's not just about cleaning the cooking pot on the outside but vigorous internal scrubbing too. The rest of this chapter will now discuss the heart of this book, the seven steps to spiritual intelligence set out in Diagram 4.2.

Step One: Setting a smart goal – ikhlas, the genuine desire to be close to God

The eleven players on a football team have a single aim of winning the match: they run, sweat, get injured, endure pain in their legs, are cheered on by the crowd or booed, but relentlessly chase the ball to score a goal. A world-class athlete sets her sights on nothing less than an Olympic gold medal or a successful entrepreneur yearns to make millions in profit. All of these people have set themselves a 'smart' goal; an acronym, S.M.A.R.T., stands for a Specific, Manageable, Achievable, Relevant and Time-bound goal. To achieve spiritual intelligence requires similar and single-minded dedication, determination and desire like that of the professional footballer, Olympic champion and the entrepreneur. By developing this attachment with our goals we become eager to achieve them and keen to succeed in making them happen. The first step in this process is an awareness that the process has begun and we have to take a conscious step in the direction of transforming ourselves.

The goal of developing spiritual intelligence is specific and well-defined, and clear enough to be recognized; it should be manageable and achievable as it's meant to be doable and not impossible, which does not mean that it won't be sometimes hard and tiresome. It can test our psychological stamina and our steadfastness and diligence, but the goal of spiritual intelligence is a realistic, relevant, practical and down-to-earth aim for us.

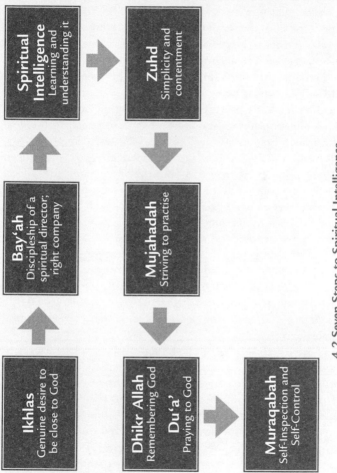

4.2 Seven Steps to Spiritual Intelligence

43

Seven Steps

There is a timescale in which spiritual intelligence has to be achieved, which is our earthly lifespan. The benefit of setting a goal for ourselves is that it acts like a lighthouse, providing us with direction, identifying the landmarks, the rocks and the resources needed to accomplish the task.

Perhaps the most important requirement after setting S.M.A.R.T. goals is being psychologically prepared, putting our trust in the Divine providence, and relying on God's generosity and kindness. Another requirement in accomplishing the goal is thorough preparation, adopting a well-tested methodology, following a well-trodden path, and adhering to a balanced training programme, which is both the Shariah and the *tariqah*. The Shariah consists of the Qur'an and the Sunnah, whilst *tariqah* is the application of it by our beloved Messenger ﷺ and the revered masters of Sufism. I equate the setting of S.M.A.R.T. goals with sincerity and genuineness of intention, or *ikhlas*, or as the Qur'an often puts it to 'genuinely seek only His pleasure' (*mukhlisina lahu al-din*). The hadiths quoted below shed more light on this concept of setting goals and will motivate us to walk confidently on this path. Personal development trainers suggest the following tips in Diagram 4.3 when setting goals to ensure that you set yourself up for success.

Sincerity or *ikhlas* is the first step on the spiritual ascent. It represents a secret conversation, a confidential dialogue and an intimate relationship between the traveller and God. It is a means of refining and illuminating the inner heart until it becomes ready to accept the good. Sincerity is one's business plan: one's intention, actions, investment and expected outcomes. 'Umar narrates that the Prophet ﷺ said, 'the value of deeds depends on the intention, for every person will get what he intended. Whoever migrated for God and the Prophet, his migration was for God and His Prophet and whoever migrated for worldly gain

Map out small, actionable steps

Divide the great goal of spiritual intelligence into seven manageable steps. At the end of each completed step, celebrate and thank God for His blessings.

Seeking help

To achieve your goal identify a spiritual director, a sheikh or teacher, who must be a qualified pious person whom you can trust.

Making Spiritual Intelligence Work for You

Make goals personal, positive and present

Prove to yourself you have achieved the goal to convince yourself to do it. Be positive about Allah, and live in His presence. What is more personal than that?

Focus on the important steps

There are many methodologies, programs and exercises to develop spiritual intelligence, but focus on the most important of these.

4.3 Making Spiritual Intelligence Work for You

or for marrying a woman, so his migration was for that purpose.' (Bukhari)

The words, 'For every person is what he intended', means that the reward for a deed is determined by one's intention: 'Whoever made *hijrah* for God and His Prophet, his *hijrah* will be considered for God and His Prophet.' *Hijrah* means to dissociate oneself, give up, abandon, surrender, or to emigrate. Its common usage is for the emigration from a land of unbelief to a Muslim country due to persecution and for the protection of one's religion. In spiritual terms, it means to give up everything that God has forbidden and separating oneself from evil and wickedness. The words 'Whoever migrates for worldly gains or for marrying a woman, his migration is for that purpose' mean that he has no reward from God. There is no share for the intender in the Hereafter if material gain or a spouse is their objective. Reward and nearness to God cannot be attained merely on the basis of outward appearance or acts alone but depend on the state of the heart or the underlying motive. Purity of intention and cleanness of the heart are essential. This is *ikhlas*. All devotion must be completely free of motives seeking worldly gains; worship must be performed faithfully and sincerely for the sake of the Almighty alone.

> The Prophet ﷺ said, 'God does not look at your bodies nor at your faces, but He looks at your hearts.' (Muslim)

Niyyah means an intention or motive. The Shariah stresses making an intention for every deed to distinguish between the routine activities of a person and the actions associated with worship. A routine activity can become an act of worship simply by making the correct intention. For example, to sit in the mosque with an intention of spiritual seclusion (*itikaf*) makes it an act of worship, but without this intention it is merely the unrewarded routine act of sitting. Similarly, if someone goes without food from dawn till dusk with the intention of fasting for God's sake, it is worship; but without such an intention, it is merely hunger and thirst without reward. These examples clearly show the enormous value of correct intention that can change mundane activities into acts of worship and become a means of achieving the God's nearness. Even eating, drinking, wearing good clothes or marriage become acts of worship if performed with the intention of pleasing God.

Step Two: Bay'ah, finding and pledging allegiance to a spiritual director

Jalaluddin Rumi advises us to 'take a guide, for without one the way is full of dangers'. For those who travel the path without a guide, how can they find the way on a path they have not travelled before? Whoever walks on an unfamiliar path without a guide falls in a well.

The way of connecting with a guide is by making an oath of allegiance (*bay'ah*), and the scholars are agreed that *bay'ah* is a Prophetic Sunnah. The Prophet ﷺ took *bay'ah* from his Companions for a variety of reasons, sometimes for *hijrah* or jihad, sometimes for the

> O prodigal! If the guide isn't there, you will be bewildered and the devils will harm you. Many cleverer than you have been misled before.
> Rumi, *Mathnawi*

regular performance of the prayer, fasting, *zakah* and pilgrimage, and sometimes he took *bay'ah* so that they would follow his Sunnah and avoid innovations. However, nowadays, it is taken for one special reason: to establish the Shariah in one's life. So this too is following the Sunnah of the blessed Messenger ﷺ. So what motivates a person to look for a sheikh? Sheikh al-'Alawi, one of the greatest Sufis of twentieth century, simply said that such a person is 'haunted by the thought of God'; in other words, they came because the clouds were not dense enough to keep out their awareness of spiritual reality, and they thirsted for the water of life.

The beloved Messenger takes bay'ah from his Companions

God has expressed His satisfaction with those people who took *bay'ah* of the Messenger ﷺ and promised a great reward for those who kept their pledge: *Surely God is pleased with those people who took your oath under the tree, He (Almighty) knows what is in their hearts so He gave them peace and tranquillity* (al-Fath 48: 18). Fifteen hundred people took an oath on the day of Hudaybiyyah. The Lord's satisfaction and the gift of peace of mind are the reward for *bay'ah*: *Whoever fulfilled his promise with God he will soon be given a great reward* (al-Fath 48:10). According to Bukhari and Muslim, all the Companions took *bay'ah*. On the day of the Battle of the Trench, the Prophet ﷺ prayed for all his Companions and they replied in unison: 'We made an oath with Muhammad for Islam and will always remain true to it.'

In the verse, *Seek a means (wasilah) unto Him* (al-Ma'idah 5: 35), the commentators interpret *wasilah* as *bay'ah*. Shah 'Abdul Rahim, the father of Shah Waliyyullah, says, 'It is impossible that *wasilah* means faith as the address is already to people of faith, and *wasilah* cannot mean 'righteous deeds' as that is implied in *taqwa*, and it cannot be jihad as that too is referred to separately.' Therefore, he concludes in *Irshad-i Rahimiyyah* that *wasilah* refers to the *bay'ah* of a spiritual guide. Abu Yazid Bustami in *Ruh al-Bayan* says, 'Whoever does not have a spiritual guide has Satan as his guide.' Abu Qasim al-Qushayri stresses the need for a sheikh in observing that, 'The tree that grows by itself without a farmer will have foliage but no fruit; we know that trees in the wild bear fruit but they do not taste the same as those grown in orchards.' Martin Lings aptly calls *wasilah* an investiture into a Sufi order in which the novice takes on the way of spiritually adept.

Step Three: Learning and understanding the nature of spiritual intelligence

The traveller on the spiritual path has to learn to purify himself physically with the ablution, about the Islamic creed, and understand morals, manners and the law. At this point, the heart is covered with rust that is a result of arrogance, greed, envy, hatred and other vices. A study of the Qur'an and the Hadith enthuses the traveller with desire to imitate the beloved Messenger 鬡.

Correct knowledge of Islam is crucial for success; this is life-enhancing knowledge that provides true awakening. It teaches the purpose of life, correct behaviour and how to avoid the temptations of the Devil; in brief, the whole art of living. This is the knowledge that makes one a dedicated servant of God, knowledge that helps our balanced growth covering all the

> The blessed Messenger 鬡 said, 'When God wishes to be kind to someone he gives him understanding of the religion.' (Muslim)

physical, spiritual, intellectual, scientific and other aspects of one's personality, and directs all of these towards goodness and the attainment of perfection. The Qur'an tells Mustafa 鬡 to pray, *Say: O my Lord! Increase my knowledge* (*Ta Ha* 20: 114).

Knowledge is like fire: once ignited, it will propagate itself. Similarly, knowledge desires more of itself. As the Qur'an says:

Are those who know and those who do not know alike? (*al-Zumar* 39: 9) Numerous hadiths also encourage the seeking of knowledge: 'Seek knowledge from the cradle to grave'; 'Whoever travels in search of knowledge, God will make his road to Paradise easy' (Muslim); and 'Cursed is the world and all that is in it except remembrance and obedience of God, the scholar and the student.' (Tirmidhi)

Step Four: Zuhd, living with simplicity and contentment

What is stopping us from realizing the existence of the spiritual realm? According to Imam Ghazali, there are two causes of this inability to see, feel and sense the 'other world': love of the world and ignorance about the reality of life. The love of the world results from our familiarity with its delights, pleasures and relationships, which slackens our desire to depart from the world and its pleasures. We become fond and eager for worldly things. We continue to think that we have our egos under control and yet our dependency on the world grows and grows. As time passes, our need for wealth, children, home, livelihood, family and friends grows, and our attachment to the world becomes ever stronger. So if anything appears as an obstacle between us and the world, it is disliked. No wonder we dislike death. If ever the thought of death comes to us, we postpone it and say to ourselves, 'We have a long time ahead of us before we get old, so we can repent then.' When we grow old, we say 'until we become very old'. And when we are very old we tell ourselves 'as soon as we finish this project' or 'free ourselves of building this or that', or 'until we return from that journey', and other such excuses. We continue to postpone and delay our repentance and fail to do good deeds. Each day new opportunities present themselves and our attachment deepens with the world until we become truly worldly. The root of all our long hopes is this love of the world.

Ignorance about our realty

The second cause of inability to see the 'other world' is sheer ignorance. Thinking we are far away from death, we don't realize that death can come us when we are young too. Our youth and good health make us complacent: we consider death to be remote when it is not. However, love of this world coupled with ignorance encourages us to develop long hopes: we attend a funeral procession but never think about our own. Imam Ghazali suggests that the way to tackle long hopes is to get rid of the love of the world. However, this can only happen if we have faith in the Day of Judgement, the day of reward and punishment, which will certainly help to diminish our love of the world. Faith in this momentous Day will wipe away our love of the inferior.

Zuhd: Turning away from the world

The Sufis understand *zuhd* as 'disliking the world and turning away from it' or 'passing over worldly pleasures to gain heavenly ones'. Imam Ahmad offers a comprehensive definition when he says, '*Zuhd* is not about making impermissible the permissible nor is it the throwing away of wealth. In fact, it is to be more certain about that which is in the Divine hands than that which is in your own hands. When a calamity afflicts you, you are full of hope for its reward, and the reward is recorded.'

Zuhd is a particular mind-set in which the person is completely reliant on Divine providence, handles the misfortunes of life confidently and positively, and is indifferent to praise and blame, a mind-set in which the world is despised and looked down upon. 'The *zahid* sees everyone as better than himself,' says Hasan al-Basri. Imam Ahmad sums up *zuhd* as 'shortening long hopes and renouncing what people possess,' in other words, worldly things are not yearned for. Imam Ahmad divides *zuhd* into three stages: (1) that of ordinary people, which is the avoidance of the Divinely forbidden things (*haram*), (2) that of special people, which is avoiding excess in permissible (*halal*) things, (3) that of the people of realization and understanding (*zuhd al-'arifin*), which is leaving everything that distracts them from the remembrance of their Lord.

The methodology and the motivation for developing zuhd

Several practices help develop *zuhd* such as reflecting on the Afterlife and standing before the Lord on Judgement Day, realizing that worldly pleasures are distractions from God, pondering the humiliation, effort and deception needed to have wealth and prestige, consideration of its fleeting nature and how small it is in God's sight. These help to control our lowly desire for worldly pleasures. The Messenger ﷺ said: 'If the world was equal in value to a mosquito's wing of a mosquito, then God would not give a sip of water to a disbeliever.' (Tirmidhi)

There are constant Qur'anic references to the world as 'a source of deception', which further strengthens the *zahid*'s belief that the world is to be avoided as much as possible. The Quran says: *Nay, you prefer the worldly life yet the Afterlife is better and everlasting* (al-A'la 16–17), and *Say! The worldly provisions are little and the afterlife is better for the God-conscious* (al-Nisa' 4: 77). Describing worldly people, the Qur'an says: *And they are happy with the worldly life and what is the worldly life compared to the Afterlife but very little* (al-Ra'd 13: 26).

Step Five: Mujahadah, striving to worship the Lord Almighty

The traveller on spiritual path has no alternative but to worship the Lord in order to develop spiritual intelligence; this is the real effort, getting up and observing night vigils! Very simply, its basics are praying devoutly, fasting in the month of Ramadan, paying *zakah* and performing the pilgrimage when ready and able to do so. God Almighty says, *We will guide to our ways those who work hard for our cause and God is with those who do good* (al-'Ankabut 29: 69).

Abu al-Qasim al-Qusharyi said, 'Remember that anyone who does not exert effort at the start of his journey on the path of God then will never receive the benefits of this path.' Iqbal writes:

> Strong faith, continuous effort and love are the conquerors
>   of the world:
> In the daily struggles of life, these are the warriors' swords.
> This is like stepping into a deadly battlefield,
> Yet people think it is easy to be a Muslim.

The path leading to nearness of God through worship is difficult. The Qur'an uses the metaphor of a steep mountain path (*'aqabah*) in *Surah al-Balad* (90: 11) to describe the difficulties of life, life being a struggle or a jihad. The above verse in *Surah al-'Ankabut* promises for those who work to make every effort to climb this steep path, those who struggle to please their Lord through worship, that they will be guided, shown the path and protected from making error or being misguided and their reward is being in the Divine presence. The verb that is used to describe this hard work and striving is *mujahadah*, which is defined as 'making the utmost effort that one is capable of to defend oneself against an enemy'. We have internal and external enemies: the internal ones are one's own will, selfishness, self-centeredness, and the lowly desires that urge us to seek pleasure. Amongst the external enemies is Satan, the arch enemy of humanity, who constantly whispers evil thoughts to us, goading us to disobey our Lord and to act against the Shariah.

The Prophet's teachings on working hard and striving in the path of God

The hadith cited earlier in this chapter about the status of God's friends ('I declare war on anyone who has enmity against My friend. ...') teaches us that the means of gaining nearness to God is following His commands. In other words, carrying out the duties that have been assigned to a believer: the daily prayers, fasting, giving charity and performing hajj. However, the friend of God who passionately loves the Lord goes beyond the call of duty and spends far more time in voluntary acts in order to please his Creator. Whilst the obligatory acts take only a small amount of time, the voluntary acts can be carried out at any or all times. Hatred of such wonderful people is a major sin so God declares war against the haters. In complete contrast, God draws close to His friends.

> The Prophet ﷺ said that God says, 'When a person comes closer to Me by a hand span, I come closer to him by a forearm's length. And when he draws nearer to Me by a forearm's length, I draw nearer to him by a full length. And when he comes walking towards Me, I go to him running.' (Bukhari)

To be inactive in God's way is due to negligence

Ibn 'Abbas relates that the Messenger ﷺ said, 'There are two gifts that people often neglect: they are health and spare time.' (Bukhari) *Ghaban* in Arabic means loss when selling or buying, and the case is similar with regards to health and spare time. If we neglect their significance, we will be losers in the Hereafter. We often neglect to take care of our bodies and same applies to time, which we waste in useless activities, the most beloved of God never did so. 'A'ishah gives us a vivid description of the Prophet's efforts: 'The Prophet ﷺ would sometimes stand in the prayer for so long that his feet would swell and I would ask him, "Why do you do this when God has forgiven your past and future errors?" And he would say, "O why should I not be a grateful servant of God?"'(Bukhari)

Motivation for Mujahadah

The following four habits help motivate us to carry out *mujahadah*:

1. *Listen to sermons and good advice*. Sermons and talks by religious leaders are powerful reminders that soften our hearts and impact upon our attitudes, leading to change. We are encouraged to have good character and shun bad behaviour.

2. *Practise and perfect good habits*. The Messenger ﷺ said that, 'Goodness is a normal habit, whilst evil wears you down. When God wishes to be kind to someone, He gives him understanding of the religion.' (Muslim)

3. *Keep the company of righteous people*. Those we keep company with have a huge influence on our lives, beliefs, attitudes and behaviour. This is why the Messenger ﷺ said, 'A man follows the religion of his friend, so be careful who you befriend.' (Muslim)

4. *Be focused*. All the distractions around us must be avoided so we can focus on our goal. The Prophet ﷺ taught us that, 'The beauty of a person's Islam lies in giving up things that do not concern him.' (Tirmidhi) The Prophet ﷺ is telling us to give up foolish or unproductive matters and focus on things

that are useful for our worldly life and our Hereafter. We should cut out gossip and useless babble too. The Prophet ﷺ advises us: 'Do not talk about things that do not concern you.' (Bukhari)

Step Six: Dhikr Allah (remembering God) and du'a' (supplicating to God)

Dhikr is God's remembrance, either with the heart or with the tongue; however, the best remembrance is done with both, and the remembrance with the heart alone is better than with the tongue alone. Imam Nawawi has endorsed this view in his famous commentary of Imam Muslim's hadith collection. He also said that the remembrance of the heart is of two kinds. The first is contemplation (*tafakkur*), which is reflection upon the creation of God. This can be the study of nature and the environment or the whole universe. This reflection leads to the reverence and awe of God as our majestic Lord and Creator, and deepens our faith in *tawhid*. As a hadith says, 'The best remembrance is reflection.' (Tabarani) The second kind of remembrance of the heart is such that the fear of the Lord prevents us from doing prohibited things and our hearts become free to remember Him, the Almighty. Remembrance is the opposite of forgetfulness, a state of mind. Hence, remembrance is the combined act of mind and tongue. God says: *And remember your Lord whenever you forget Him* (al-Kahf 18: 24).

The virtues of dhikr

God says: *Remember me and I shall remember you* (al-Baqarah 2: 152). The blessed Messenger ﷺ also relates that God Almighty says, 'I am as my servant thinks of Me and I am with him when he remembers Me. When he remembers Me within himself, I remember him within Myself. When he mentions me in an assembly, I mention him in a better assembly....' (Bukhari and Muslim) On another occasion, the Prophet ﷺ urged his Companions to engage in remembrance constantly: 'Remember God frequently until people say that you are mad!' (Ahmad) Once the Messenger ﷺ said to them, 'Renew your faith!' They asked, 'How do we renew our faith, O Messenger of God?' He answered, 'Say: "There is no god but God (*la ilaha illallah*)" in abundance for its trail allows no sin to remain, no other deed resembles it and no veil comes between it and God.' (Tirmidhi) At another time he said, 'When you pass by the meadows of Paradise, then graze in them.' Someone asked, 'O Messenger of God, what are the meadows of Paradise?' He replied, 'The circles of remembrance.' (Muslim)

The Sufi masters stress the impact and excellence of remembrance of the heart; it negates everything other than God. In other words, the love of God and *tawhid* should replace the love of all other things. This is the whole purpose of remembrance. There are four ways of remembering God: (1) with the tongue while the heart is forgetful, which is a poor form of remembrance; (2) with the tongue and the heart, but it is not fully established in the heart and demands more effort; (3) with the heart fully engaged such that it is not distracted, which is a wonderful state; and (4) thoughts of God are dominant such that one cannot distinguish between the remembrance and the Remembered. The heart is full of love and is unaware of the remembrance; it is engrossed in the Remembered, and this is the real remembrance.

The keys to answered prayer

The Qur'an constantly motivates us to pray to God: *Call on Me and I will answer you* (*Ghafir* 40: 60). Muhammad ibn 'Ulan in his commentary on Imam Nawawi's *Riyad al-Salihin* notes that the glorious Qur'an uses the term *du'a'* for a variety of meanings such as devotion, seeking help, asking for something, word, call and praise. Fakhr al-Din al-Razi in *Tafsir al-Kabir* defines *du'a'* as 'the pleading of the servant to the Lord for support, help and provision'. *Du'a'* refers to a sincere call, an earnest appeal and humble request, which the worshipper makes to his majestic Lord. This 'call' could be for help at a time of difficulty, for Divine benevolence or for consolation and peace of mind. This gives the believer a sense of self-assurance, making us feel secure, a priceless gift in our turbulent times. Is it any wonder then why the Messenger ﷺ said: *'Du'a' is the essence of worship'*, as there is deep concentration in supplication, the mind does not wonder about, the imagination is focused without distractions, and there is a hypnotic stillness as we focus on some remembered concern relevant to our supplication or a Qur'anic phrase. When we are engrossed in supplication there is an absorption in the Divine so that our other faculties are mesmerized.

The significance of du'a'

One of the Divine names is al-Mujib, the One who answers and replies to the call of his servants: *Call on Me and I will answer you* (*Ghafir* 40: 60). *Du'a'* is not only a form of remembrance of the Lord but is also a pleasant experience. It generates spiritual energy that comforts the soul, is the coolness of the eye and gives peace of mind. The Messenger ﷺ likened one who remembers God to a living person full of energy and vitality; on the other hand, he likened the forgetful person to a corpse. A central verse on *du'a'* is: *When my servants ask you about Me, surely I am near. I answer the caller when he calls Me, so let them obey Me and believe in Me so they may be guided* (*al-Baqarah* 2: 186), acceptance meaning satisfaction with the Divine will, but this is negated when the supplicant prefers his or her own wish over that of the Divine will. Salman Farsi says that 'Your Lord is very modest and generous: when a person raises his hand and asks Him something, He does not return them empty-handed.' (Abu Dawud) He discusses the excellence of *du'a'* and says: 'In supplication, there is no intermediary between man and the Lord: it is a direct dialogue.'

How to make a supplication

Here are the basic manners of supplication:

1. Sit calmly and in a composed manner facing the Kaaba. Raise both hands close your face with the cupped palms facing heavenwards at the level of your shoulders. After completing your supplication, wipe both hands on the face. 'Umar said, 'The Messenger 鹵 never lowered his hands without wiping his face after supplication.' (Tirmidhi)

2. Open and close the supplication by sending blessings on the Messenger 鹵, then adore and praise the Lord, followed by contrition, seeking forgiveness for your sins, then thank God for His boundless generosity, until finally you are ready to supplicate, and present your plea. The acronym A.C.T.S. (Adoration, Contrition, Thanks, Supplication) captures these steps of calling on the Lord in supplication.

3. In supplication, be humble, gentle and patient and full of hope that the Lord will accept your prayer.

4. It is sinful to make prayers which are about severing ties, breaking up relationships or asking for Divine help to commit a crime.

Step Seven: Muraqabah, vigilant awareness

The Arabic noun *muraqabah* is derived from the verb *raqaba,* which means to observe carefully or to keep a careful eye on something. In Sufism, *muraqabah* means 'to develop consciousness of one's sins and to become self-critical so that one can avoid sins that prevent love of the Divine, sacrifice and sincerity from taking hold in the heart.' The English equivalents of *muraqabah* are self-examination, introspection and contemplation. Imam Abu Qasim al-Qushayri quotes al-Juryari as saying, 'Our way is founded on two parts: that you compel your self to be vigilantly aware of God and to make this be visible in your outward behaviour.' Ibrahim al-Khawwas said, 'Observance leads to vigilant observance that leads to inner and outer devotion to God Most High.' Vigilant observance gives one internal silence and rest, clearing the clutter in one's mind and providing a sense of calm that helps one to connect realistically with the world around you. Abu 'Uthman said, 'When you sit instructing the people, be a preacher to your own heart and self first of all, and do not allow people around you to deceive you that they only interested in your outward behaviour, while God watches your inner being.'

Muraqabah as mentioned in the Sunnah

The blessed Messenger ﷺ used to spend a lot of time in the Cave of Hira' in stillness and solitude high above the city of Makkah. He contemplated and prepared himself mentally and spiritually for the heavy task of preaching. However, he loved to teach, preach and be with his Companions as well.

The vigilant person is careful about his or her attitudes and actions and guards both heart and mind. The Prophet ﷺ ordered us to 'Fear God wherever you are, follow a bad deed with a good one to wipe it away, and behave well towards people.' (Tirmidhi)

This made the Companions very sensitive about their dealings with people. The Companion Anas ibn Malik advising his students said, 'You do things that are trivial in

> The Prophet ﷺ said, 'The intelligent person is the one who controls himself and works for the Hereafter, and the foolish person is the one who follows his whims yet hopes for God's mercy.' (Tirmidhi)

your eyes, yet in the time of the Messenger we regarded them as appalling sins.' (Bukhari)

KEY POINTS

❈ Active learning is much more effective than passive learning in taking steps to spiritual intelligence.

❈ The seven steps to spiritual intelligence are genuine seeking of God, discipleship of a spiritual director, learning and understanding spiritual intelligence, simplicity and contentment, striving to practise, remembering and praying to God, self-inspection and self-control.

Chapter Five

The Ranks of Spiritual Intelligence: Charting the Spiritual Journey

This chapter charts the progress the seeker of spiritual intelligence makes. These are the famous seven ranks described by spiritual masters, as one progresses from the uncouth and degenerate self to the highly-developed self, the perfected self that possesses self-realization and inward knowledge of God.

I have based this chapter on a small but authoritative book *The Degrees of the Soul* by Sheikh 'Abd al-Khaliq al-Shabrawi al-Azhari (d.1947), which provides an account of the various sicknesses of the self and their remedies (*tazkiyah*). These are the sicknesses that prevent the heart from perceiving the Unseen, and the remedies include various devotional practices and self-discipline that have been discussed in previous chapters. Al-Shabrawi describes the seven ranks of spiritual intelligence, outlining their characteristics and what the seeker may experience in each rank.

The author argues that the whole purpose of travelling on this journey is to acquire perfection by getting rid of blameworthy characteristics and acquiring praiseworthy ones. On the path of spirituality, the traveller become pure by removing all traces of evil and does this by following the Sunnah meticulously. Enjoying luxuries and worldly pleasures and gratifying the appetites cover the heart with rust, or veils it. As the heart controls the whole body, a rusty heart props up evil as it is overpowered by passion: the heart that was once the ruler has now become the conquered and dejected prisoner and subject. The longer the self is in this miserable position, it fails to focus on the meaning and purpose of life and continues to sin until 'the heart becomes rusty like iron becomes rusty'. Someone asked the Prophet ﷺ, 'What will remove it?' He replied, 'The remembrance of death and the recitation of the Qur'an.' (Abu Dawud)

Al-Shabrawi describes the self as the vital force that keeps the human body alive, and he identifies its seven developmental ranks. Each rank has its own particular competences and abilities, which increase as the self is refined and comes closer to its Lord:

The lowest rank is the inciting self: this is the passionate self, the bestial human, full of anger, hatred, jealousy, greed, arrogance, pride and conceit. There is very little goodness or spiritual intelligence. When it submits to the Shariah and agrees to follow the truth, it continues to be attracted to worldly pleasures and indulges in wretchedness. Its attempt to live by the Shariah is a struggle; however, its inner yearning and the encouragement from external sources like friends or a sheikh motivates it to continue on the straight path. As it does so, it begins to see its own shortcomings and becomes self-critical, which is the reproachful self. As the attraction for worldly pleasures decreases and the longing for devotion increases, it is accompanied by the wish to act righteously. The agitations quieten and the passions lose their grip over the self and it begins to forget its pleasures altogether: the reproachful self becomes the serene self. As it continues its upward journey, it ascends the spiritual ranks until it becomes the contented self, and then the self found pleasing, such that it is pleasing both to its Lord and His creatures. When

Ranks

The Third Rank
The Inspired Self
(al-nafs al-mulhamah)

The Fourth Rank
The Serene Self
(al-nafs al-mutma'innah)

The Second Rank
The Reproachful Self
(al-nafs al-lawwamah)

The Fifth Rank
The Contented Self
(al-nafs al-radiyah)

The First Rank
The Inciting Self
(al-nafs al-ammarah)

The Sixth Rank
The Self Found Pleasing
(al-nafs al-mardiyyah)

The Seventh Rank
The Perfected Self
(al-nafs al-kamilah)

5.1 The Seven Ranks of Spiritual Intelligence

the self is given the command by its Lord to return to created beings to guide and perfect them, it is called the perfected self.

Rank One: The inciting self (al-nafs al-ammarah)

The only way to come out of this wretched and miserable state of the inciting self is through repentance. The Messenger ﷺ said, 'The one who repents from his sin is like the one who is sinless; repentance removes whatever has preceded it.' The major veil of sins between the servant and the Lord is removed, he now perceives that which is from God as he becomes fearful of punishment and hopeful of mercy. Progressing from the inciting to the reproachful self requires constant and continuous effort, as it is under the sway of worldly things and unable to differentiate between right and wrong. While Satan still has influence over it, spiritual exercises like fasting, the night vigil, restricting speech, limiting interaction with people, remembrance of God, deep reflection, eating halal and avoiding forbidden things ensures that the inciting self loses its grip and is transformed into the reproachful self. Al-Shabrawi recommends abandoning procrastination and laziness, doing good and abandoning the abandoning the fleeting pleasures of the flesh. One's quest is to get rid of all blameworthy characteristics mentioned above, such as pride, ostentation and hatred, and to seek humility and the love of others instead.

Rank Two: The reproachful self (al-nafs al-lawwamah)

It is characterized by being reproachful; it is critical of itself and others and full of secret desire for glory and fame. There are still remnants of the inciting self in it. However, it acknowledges truth as truth and falsehood as falsehood. There is still a sense of seeking pleasure, it loves to be admired for its righteousness, but getting rid of this would lead to sincerity. At this rank, the traveller perceives himself as having created his own actions and therefore lacks sincerity in them because he does not see that God Most Exalted is the Creator of all acts. He is therefore likely to complain and be weary and miserable due to conceit, arrogance, rancour and bad character. He may also be engrossed in unlawful earnings and other such things that inevitably lead to difficulty and anxiety. At this rank of spiritual intelligence, there is acceptance by God but the traveller is unable to rid himself of all blemishes and to become pious. By practising the Prophet's prescriptions, such as fasting, the traveller is able to fight Satan's whispers and other evil thoughts. To progress from the second rank to the third, the traveller needs the guidance of a spiritual guide, and it is only God who grants success.

Rank Three: The inspired self (al-nafs al-mulhamah)

In this rank, the traveller pays attention to God alone as the reality of faith has dawned on him. His spiritual intelligence is growing rapidly, and everything other than God has become trivial in his eyes. The characteristics of this rank are complete submission to God, knowledge, forgiving people, inviting them to do good, willingness to accept their excuses and accepting the fact that God indeed controls everything. These positive qualities are expressed in behaviour like weeping, agitation and the absence of fear and hope and enjoyment of singing and being moved to ecstasy, loving the remembrance of God, having joy in the presence of others, preaching words of wisdom, and knowledge and creative vision. This is the inspired self: it is the territory of combat and warfare. At this rank, the angels inspire and Satan whispers. The inspired self is not fully developed and is trapped between the angels and Satan. It is still in danger of plummeting to 'the lowest of the low' back to the rank of the inciting self, with all its evil traits, and that is why the path to the rank of perfection is so precarious. Although some of the veils are stripped away and have disappeared, others still remain intact. The inspired self is in crucial need of guidance from a spiritual director, a sheikh.

The inspired self is the first degree of perfection: the traveller has abandoned trivia and deception and is ever more ready to pray, fast and isolate himself from others. However, if the traveller is unable to find a spiritual guide then he must follow the Shariah meticulously, carrying out daily routines scrupulously in following the Prophet's Sunnah. The traveller with an inspired self has the ability to overcome evil and the reality of faith and certainty are well and alive. Several of the thickest veils and most evil desires have been lifted from the traveller's heart and have disappeared.

Rank Four: The serene self (al-nafs al-mutma'innah)

At the fourth rank, the traveller does not deviate from the legal injunctions of the Shariah and takes pleasure in following the Prophet's Sunnah. The serene self has mastery over itself, controls the senses and has certainty of faith. The traveller's spiritual intelligence is now a source of delight for others who listen when he speaks and are not bored by him. His tongue is able to express the words that God casts in his mind and he speaks with the authority of a true follower of the Prophet ﷺ. He must now sit with people, guiding, teaching and inspiring them. However, he must not forget his *dhikr* and contemplation, so that he can journey to the next blessed rank.

The spiritual routine (*wird*) for this rank is the Real (al-Haqq), one of the names of God. At the fourth rank, the traveller likes to sing litanies, invocations, prayers and poems in praise of the beloved Messenger ﷺ. As he desires money only to assist others in serving God and helping others, this is a noble intention; he does not become distracted by earning money nor does he keep it secretly. A desire for leadership, to be a sheikh who guides others may arise, but beware as it is a trick of the ego. If God wishes one to become a guide, the sign of this is that one's brothers seek such guidance and company. The serene self does not see itself as better than others but only its debts to them, and guides others gently, respecting them and teaching them to love the path. It thanks God Who has raised the serene self to this position for which it is indebted to its Lord. It experiences serenity from the Merciful, follows the Book, the Sunnah and the Shariah, and contemplates the beauty and the majesty of the Real.

Rank Five: The contented self (al-nafs al-radiyah)

The fifth rank is that of extinction of the self (*fana'*), extinction means ridding oneself of human weaknesses. Extinction is followed by gaining and becoming firm in the truth of certainty (*haqq al-yaqin*), that is having true faith. The contented self discerns the truth of certainty experientially; however, a spiritual guide who has reached the rank of perfection may be able to explain it to the traveller.

Some of the characteristics of the contented self are detachment from everything other than God Most Exalted, sincerity, scrupulousness, contentedness and acceptance of everything that occurs in the universe without the heart objecting. This contented self is absorbed in the contemplation of absolute beauty. As the traveller's spiritual intelligence grows, he guides and counsels people who benefit immensely from his wisdom. The contented self is immersed in an ocean of courtesy of the Exalted: its prayers are never rejected yet it never asks for favours. It is honoured, favoured and trusted by the people, as though God's creatures are obliged to show respect to it.

The spiritual routine for this fifth rank of spiritual intelligence is al-Hayy, the Ever-Living, the One Who possesses all life and is free from death. The contented self repeats the *wird* abundantly so that extinction departs and is replaced by subsistence by the Ever-Living. At this rank, other beautiful names of God that are uttered and whose meaning is truly understood are: al-Wahhab, the One Who gives without being asked; al-Fattah, the Opener, the One Who opens the treasures of His mercy for all His servants; and al-Wahid, the One in Whose essence there is no multiplicity.

Rank Six: The self found pleasing (al-nafs al-mardiyyah)

This rank of the self is called 'found pleasing' because God is pleased with it. The characteristics of spiritual intelligence at this sixth rank are: intense focus on the Lord Most Exalted, moral character, gentleness to others, guiding them to the straight path, forgiving their mistakes, loving them and wanting to nurture and develop them too. The traveller at this rank keeps his promise and spends generously and appropriately. While others may think him being profligate or spendthrifty, the traveller always keeps to the middle course in all affairs, which is something that only the self found pleasing or perfected can do. He is now truly a representative of God (*khalifat Allah*). This is the investiture of 'I am his hearing with which he hears, his eyes with which he sees, his hand with which he strikes, and his feet with which he walks' for it is by the Real that he hears, by Him that he sees, by Him that he strikes, and by Him that he walks. All evil and wickedness are reprehensible to the self found pleasing, and it is spurred to goodness of all kinds, and is active in voluntary prayers and self-discipline. The *wird* of this rank is al-Qayyum, the Sustainer, the One who constantly sustains creation and runs its affairs.

Rank Seven: The perfected self (al-nafs al-kamilah)

The traveller has now perfected his spiritual intelligence and has no desire other than the good pleasure of his Lord: his movements are acts of goodness, every breath is an act of worship, and when people see him they are reminded of God. How could it be otherwise when he is God's perfected friend and His true representative? He constantly worships his Lord with his whole body, tongue and heart, humbly seeking forgiveness, yet is full of joy and delight when created beings turn towards their Lord, and feels sorrow and anger when they turn away from Him. He loves the seeker of truth more than his own child. There is no hatred, rancour, anger or greed in him; however, he still shows aversion when it is deserved and fears no one when speaking for God. All he wants is al-Haqq, the Real. His prayers, pleas and desires are answered by his Lord immediately. The *wird* of this rank is the name al-Qahhar, the Compeller, the One who imposes His wish on creation and no one can resist it.

KEY POINTS

❀ The seven ranks of the self as the inciting self, then the reproachful self, then the inspired self, then the serene self, then the contented self, then the self found pleasing and finally the perfected self.

❀ Climbing through the ranks of spiritual intelligence is a dynamic process: one can only begin with repentance and constant spiritual effort, but there is always the danger of slipping back, especially at the lowest two ranks.

❀ The guidance of a true spiritual director is very critical to having success, but if none is available then following the Sunnah meticulously is a must.

Chapter Six

The Fruits of Spiritual Intelligence: Love of God and Strong Character

Spirituality is the prevailing perspective on life that profoundly influences our moral and social lives. It produces spiritually intelligent people who are the best in society. This chapter describes the luscious fruits of spiritual intelligence that characterize the best of humanity: the love of God and moral character that serves and benefits others.

Al-Wadud, the Loving, is one of the Divine names. The Qur'an says: *And seek your Lord's forgiveness and then turn to Him. Indeed my Lord is merciful and loving (al-Tawbah 9: 90).* God's love of His creation is variously expressed through His other attributes too such as the Merciful (al-Rahman), the Forgiving (al-Ghafur), the Patient (al-Sabur) and so forth. In this chapter, I focus on man's love of God in which the Divine is the object of human love. The Quran and the Hadith emphasize the significance of loving God, a love manifested by Muslim scholars and Sufis in all ages. The Qur'an alludes to the profound and the intense love of the believers for *those who believe love God intensely (al-Baqarah 2: 165).*

What are the marks of Divine love?

Love itself is used to describe several emotions like amiability, warmth and tenderness, but, in a more profound sense, like maternal love, it is in the words of T.E. Jessop 'chiefly a structure of the whole mind, the entire personality moulded to a certain shape, tilted to a massive bias, organised to think, feel, desire and act in a certain way towards a certain object.'

So what are the characteristic features of the lover of God? The Prophet 鈴 says, 'Whoever possesses three qualities will taste the flavour of true faith: that God and his Prophet are dearer to him than anything else; that a person loves another purely for the sake of God; and that he dislikes returning to the state of disbelief as he would dislike being thrown into the blazing Fire.' (Bukhari and Muslim) This 'intense love of God' leads to Divine proximity, and closeness and strong bonding with God. The following hadith describes how this highest of spiritual fruits is attained: 'My servant draws near to Me by carrying out obligatory duties and then continues to draw nearer to Me through voluntary acts until I love him. ...' So being engrossed in devotions like prayer, fasting, charity and other good disciplines is a clear sign of loving God. Love being mutual, God reciprocates and protects the senses of Divine lovers: his or her hearing, seeing, and other capabilities are all taken care of by God. Nor does He keep the name of His friend and beloved secret for, as a tradition says, 'When God loves someone, Gabriel is informed of this and told to love him, so he loves him too and announces it amongst the heavenly angels that so-and-so is God's beloved, so love him! And so they love him too and then his acceptance is also established for the people on earth.' (Bukhari) Rumi likens the human yearning for the Divine to the lament of a flute separated from its reed bed, a symbol of the human soul's sorrow at being separated from its beloved Lord:

Listen to this flute, how it complains, telling a tale of
   separation;

'Ever since I was cut off from my reed bed, all have
   lamented my bewailing.

I want the breast torn asunder so as to reveal the agony
   of my yearning.

Everyone who has been separated from its origin longs to
   be united with it.'

God is to be loved more than anyone or anything else

All Muslims agree that loving God and his Messenger is
mandatory: in fact, it is the very purpose of human creation. A
heart empty of this love is dead. To develop this love, various
devotions and rituals have been instituted, as the Lord says: *I
created man and jinn only for my worship* (al-Dhariyat 51: 56). Without
the Divine love, worship is tasteless and as love is very reason for
worship it surpasses it in significance. This love further deepens
faith as the Qur'an says: *Those who believe are deeply in love with
God* (al-Baqarah 2: 165). The Messenger 🌸 makes this love a
requirement and precondition of true faith when he says: 'None
of you can be a believer until he loves God and His Messenger
more than anything else' and 'None of you can be a believer
until I am dearer to him then his father, children and all people.'
(Bukhari and Muslim) This reflects the Qur'an's teaching too:
*Say if your fathers, children, brothers, wives, relatives, your hard-earned
wealth, the business about whose damage you are always apprehensive, the
house you love, (if all these worldly things) are more dear to you than God,
His Messenger and jihad in His path, wait for the (severe) punishment that
will be meted out* (al-Tawbah 9: 24). The love of God includes the
love of the Messengers, the Companions and the friends (*awliya'*)
of God. The love of God is practically illustrated by following and
obeying the Messenger 🌸: *Say! If you love God then follow me and God*

will love you and forgive your sins (Al 'Imran 3: 31).

The Prophet ﷺ yearned for the Divine love. He used to pray: 'O Lord! Give me Your love and the love of him who loves You and works that will lead to Your love. O God! Make Your love dearer to me than myself and family and cold water.' (Tirmidhi) A man once asked, 'O Messenger! When will Judgement Day come?' He replied, 'What have you prepared for it?' The man replied, 'I haven't got many prayers and fasts to my credit but I passionately love God and His Messenger.' He replied, 'You will be those whom you love.' (Muslim)

Why do you love someone?

Hafiz 'Abdul Karim (d.1938), a Sufi saint of the Punjab, teaches that there are four rational reasons for love. The first is that a person naturally loves himself, struggles for survival, and hates anything that will harm him. Yet if a person loves himself, he must also love Him who has given him life and sustains him at every moment, so how can a person not love his Creator (al-Khaliq) and Sustainer (Rabb)? There is no escaping loving God. The second reason is that a person loves someone else as he may benefit from his wealth, support and protection from harm. Yet it is God Who is the real Provider (al-Razzaq) and Protector (al-Muhaymin) of humanity; all others are relative and secondary. Again, there is no escaping loving God. The third reason is that a person loves someone else for their moral virtues or physical beauty, yet it is God Who creates these virtues in people and makes them beautiful, so again there is no escaping loving God. The final reason is that a person loves someone else for their knowledge and power. Yet all accumulated knowledge is tiny compared to with the All-Knowing (al-'Alim) and All-Powerful (al-Qayyum). If all the brilliant scientists were to collaborate to make a mosquito, they could not do so as humanity's knowledge and power is limited, but God's is unlimited, so again there is no escaping loving God. As the Messenger ﷺ said: 'I cannot praise You enough; You are as You have described Yourself.' (Muslim)

Spiritual intelligence spurs the development of strong character. As explained in Chapter 1, spiritual intelligence is the knowledge of the meaning and purpose of life, and undertaking practices that enhance connection with God and helps us to be God's representatives on earth. Its acquisition produces personal and moral development that leads to inward and outward happiness. This is the knowledge through which one attains Divine love, purification of the self and ridding oneself of moral vices and developing moral virtues. The fruits of spiritual intelligence are love of God and moral character, for, as the Prophet ﷺ said, 'Religion is morality.' This does not mean religion is *only* morality, but its pre-eminence in Islam is being emphasized here. Morality is not a particular act but the desire to act righteously – it is a mind-set energized and powered by spiritual intelligence, and, as such, moral acts are a sign of applying spiritual intelligence to the inner will.

What is strong character?

Ghazali says that 'morality is a firmly established condition', a disposition that is well-entrenched in its possessor, something that, as we say, 'goes all the way down', unlike a habit such as being a tea drinker. A disposition is multi-track, unlike a single-track propensity such as honesty. It is also concerned with emotions, reactions, choices, values, desires, perceptions, attitudes, interests, expectations and sensibilities. For a person to possess a morality is to have moral character and a dedicated mind-set. Moral character is a principle of human nature, and, as a principle, it is real, effective, purposeful and meaningful. It is like a lighthouse, a permanent source of illumination and guidance that warns the traveller of the dangers and the vast unknown land that lies ahead.

Moral character built on the foundations of spiritual intelligence leads to honesty, compassion, justice, courage, gentleness, forgiveness, humility, modesty, generosity and patience. By themselves, neither human reason nor nature can provide the foundations for morality, as this spiritual connection and faith in God is required. For humanity to be selfless, it must have spiritual intelligence to acknowledge the Divine source of grace and power outside itself that provides a solid foundation for morality.

KEY POINT

❀ The two outstanding fruits of spiritual intelligence are the love of God and a strong moral character.

Chapter Seven

The Masters of Spiritual Intelligence: The Friends of God

Faith has a lot to do with the fact that there are wonderful and trustworthy people around us, richly endowed with spiritual intelligence. They are the friends of God (*awliya' Allah*), completely dedicated to God's service and close to Him. They are prepared to live and die and love and hate for His sake. Their motto is *My prayers, my sacrifices, life and death are all for the Lord of universe* (*al-An'am* 6: 162). They are living proof of God, signs of God (*ayat Allah*), who display His generosity and make His compassion tangible in the world. The Qur'an praises them, saying *Surely the friends of God will have nothing to fear nor grieve over* (*Yunus* 10: 62). They are people who take God, His Prophet and His religion seriously in contrast to those who consider their religion a thing of play and amusement. Muslims trust these friends of God, and love them. Love of God starts by being impressed by these friends of God and developing trust in them, the starting point of Divine love. As our relationship with them develops, we want to live like they live and follow them.

The Quran's description of God's friends

God says: *Beware! The friends of God are fearless and they shall not grieve, they are strong in faith and ever God-conscious. For them is good news of happiness in this life and the Hereafter. Nothing can alter the Divine promise: this is supreme success* (*Yunus* 10: 62–64). This short passage reveals the affection and love that God has for His friends. A friend is someone who enjoys mutual affection and regard exclusive of family relationships. The Arabic noun *waliyy*, which is derived from the verb *waliya*, means near or close, friend, helper or patron. There are two types of nearness. Firstly, 'universal nearness', which everything, a human being or an atom, has with its Creator. God says: *We are nearer to you than your jugular vein* (*Qaf* 50:16). Secondly, 'special nearness', which is the Divine love granted to select people, and it has many degrees. Its two basic conditions are faith and piety. What does it mean to be near to God? Imam Razi says in *Tafsir al-Kabir*, 'Nearness to God in terms of space or direction is impossible; nearness to God is when the heart is gripped by Divine love. When one observes one sees the signs of God's power, when one listens one hears the Divine verses, when one speaks one sings the Divine praises, when one stirs one moves in worship, when one struggles and strives one does so in obeying God.'

Why are God's friends important for us?

These people live simple yet effective and impressive lives. Their contribution to Islam is that they have taken on the responsibility of making Islam and God credible in the world. Their whole lives are a testament to the love, mercy and greatness of God. They are witnesses for the Divine truth, they follow the Prophets, resist the evils of society, and possess outstanding characteristics of devotion and service. We can be cynical about others: why should we believe in someone? Why should we trust someone? We believe people have hidden agendas. As we cannot uncover the hidden motives of others, we mistrust them. However, God's friends are different: they have no hidden agenda or self-interest, seeking neither glory nor praise nor recognition. Their pure and selfless lives are as transparent as glass: we can see right through them! They have nothing to hide and reveal all, so much so that the Prophet ﷺ said, 'When you see them they remind you of God.' Through the lives of God's friends, God is no longer remote. What is hidden is revealed and He becomes near and Real. In Islam, the Prophet ﷺ occupies the highest rank of Divine friendship, followed by the four great prophets (Ibrahim, Nuh, Musa and Jesus), then the other prophets. The prophets are followed by the Companions like Abu Bakr and others. This galaxy of God's illustrious friends, the shining stars of humanity and perfected human beings are unique, special and peerless. There are other friends of God drawn from the Muslim community, who have acquired nearness to God, so much so that they are absorbed in the Divine. They are our guides. They point to God, and their lives appeal to us. They have traversed the seven steps and ranks of spiritual intelligence, described in previous chapters. They have a personal and intimate relationship with God. This personal relationship with His friends is variously described in the Quran vividly, and, in particular, with the Prophets. Take our beloved Prophet Muhammad ﷺ, whose life is key to understanding the nature and intentions of God. He embodied, lived and practised the beautiful attributes of God: the complete beauty and grandeur of God shone from his character. Similarly, the friends of God are the representatives of God.

The signs of God's friends

There is a beautiful hadith that gives us insight into the lives of these wonderful people of spiritual intelligence. Someone once asked the Prophet ﷺ: 'Who are friends of God?' He said, 'When you look at them they remind you of God.' (Bayhaqi) They have attained spiritual intelligence and their hearts are polished so they reflect the Divine beauty and goodness, just like a mirror reflects rays of light. Their humility, devotion and absorption in worship remind us of the Hereafter. I have selected the following five stars of Sufism as they represent these spiritually intelligent beings who were successful in guiding and educating others in this path.

Sheikh Abu 'Abd al-Rahman al-Sulami (d. 1021)

He was born in 937 in Nishapur, a city in north-eastern Iran. He is an important early writer on Sufism, particularly its formative period. He was jurist of the Shafiʻi legal school who had mastery over many fields of Islamic learning. One reason for his substantial influence is that he had many outstanding students and disciples like Abu Qasim al-Qushayri, Abu Nuʻaym al-Isfahani and Imam al-Bayhaqi. He was particularly interested in Sufism and his greatest legacy are his works *The Stations of the Righteous* and *The Stumbling of the Aspirants*, which give us access to Sufi spiritual methods and teachings the of masters, as well as giving us insights into the principles, attitudes and practices of the Sufis in his day. His contemporaries praised al-Sulami for his integrity, for instance, that 'He is one of those we have encountered who have devoted themselves completely to the precepts and disciplines of Sufism in accordance with that which the founders based their path upon, rightly guided by their example, steadfast on their path, following in their footsteps, and dissociating himself from all the deranged and confused among the ignorant of these factions, totally disclaiming them.' Al-Sulami's student al-Khashshab (d.1063) praises his ability to be in harmony with all of those around him: 'He was well considered by the elect and the masses, with those in accord (with his views), and with those against, with the sultan and with the subjects, in his own country, and in all the Islamic countries; and thus he passed from this world onto God.'

Imam Abu Hamid al-Ghazali (d. 1111)

Known as the Proof of Islam (Hujjat al-Islam), he was born in 1058 in Tabran, a town in north-eastern Persia. As his father was a cotton merchant, he is referred to as Ghazali. His early education came from teachers in his hometown; later, he then moved to Jurjan and studied under Imam Abu Nasr Isma'ili. The young Ghazali was a brilliant student with an incisive wit and a sharp intellect. Among the many centres of learning, Nishapur and Baghdad were the most famous. As Nishapur was closer to home, Ghazali decided to go there and study under Imam Juwayni (d.1086), regarded as the greatest scholar of the day. As the grand mufti, he was highly esteemed by the government and the public. Ghazali excelled and soon earned a special place amongst the Imam's students and was appointed as his assistant teacher. Ghazali was encouraged by his teacher to write, and his fame spread soon spread. It was around this time that he was initiated in the spiritual order of Sheikh Farmadi.

Ghazali then headed to the Nizamiyyah College in Baghdad to university of Nizamiyyah was appointed as a teacher at this prestigious institution. The College's patron, the ruler Nizam al-Mulk, was an erudite scholar himself who loved the company of scholars: his court was like a debating society. This provided young scholars with an opportunity to show off their debating skills and depth of scholarship and impress the royals. Ghazali loved the pomp and ceremony of these occasions, and it wasn't long before his genius in debating, lecturing and counselling and his brilliance in all branches of learning – philosophy, law, apologetics and spirituality – became apparent. Recognizing this, Nizam al-Mulk appointed Ghazali, at only the age of thirty-four, as the head of the Nizamiyyah, a high-ranking civil appointment and the most coveted seat of learning in Baghdad, the capital of the Muslim empire. He now had a lot of influence on the royal family, and his fame, riches, reputation and influence were at their peak.

Yet despite this environment of wealth and fame, Ghazali's interest in spirituality developed and he became critical of his own love of pomp, wealth and status. An inner conflict grew within him: he was increasingly sceptical about his academic position and his relationship with wealthy and worldly people. He felt like leaving Baghdad to retreat into the wilderness. 'For six months,' Ghazali writes in his autobiography, 'I was in a state of tremendous anxiety until I could not speak, nor eat, nor teach. Eventually, I became ill; physicians declared me untreatable.' He continues, 'I came to the conclusion that the blessings of the Hereafter cannot be attained without *taqwa* and giving up carnal desires. And this can only happen once the love of the world disappears, until one renounces the world and yearns for the Hereafter. Man must energetically and completely turn to his Lord. And this cannot happen without giving up pomp and wealth. When I examined myself, I found myself deeply attached to the world. When I studied the motives behind my lecturing I found it was merely for grandeur and status. I was now convinced that I stood at the brink of disaster. I reflected on this state for a long time. One day I would decide to leave Baghdad and free myself of these shackles but the next day I would change my mind.

I would take one step forward and another backward. In the morning I would yearn for the Hereafter but by the evening those thoughts would be overwhelmed by worldly desires. The chains of carnal desires would pull me and the voice of faith would say, "Go! Go! Only a few hours of life remain yet the journey is long, your works are merely for showing off and delusion. If you do not prepare for the Hereafter now, when will you do so?" Finally, I decided to leave Baghdad. The scholars and the government officials pleaded to me to take back my decision saying, "This will be bad luck for the Muslims; how can your departure be justifiable?" Whilst everyone was saying this, I knew the truth and therefore left for Syria.'

Ghazali travelled to Damascus and lived in solitude, spending his time in devotion and self-purification and busying himself with developing his spiritual intelligence. He would climb the western minaret of the Grand Umayyad Mosque of Damascus and remain there all day immersed in Divine remembrance, and would also teach in the Grand Mosque's western wing. After two years of devotion and spiritual exercises, he moved to Jerusalem and stayed at the Dome of the Rock. From there, he went to Khalil, a town in the West Bank near the tomb of Prophet Ibrahim ﷺ, where he made three pledges: to never to visit a royal court, accept royal gifts or debate with anyone. From there, he decided to perform the pilgrimage to Makkah. For ten long years he remained on his journey of self-discovery and the search for truth: wondering through deserts, jungles, cities and mountains, and often staying near the tombs of God's friends, Imam Ghazali wrote, taught at seminaries and guided students. After this intense spiritual journeying, he thereafter returned to Baghdad, where he was received with joy and offered again the headship of the Nizamiyyah. It is thought that it was at this point that he wrote his magnum opus *The Revival of the Religious Sciences*, a classic of Islamic scholarship. For the first time, he combined the legal aspects of the Shariah with its inner dimensions of morality and spirituality. Ghazali only taught at the Nizamiyyah for a short while before returning to his hometown, where he established a small seminary. He continued to write until his death at the age of fifty-three. His younger brother Ahmad gives an account of his last day: 'On Monday morning, the Imam woke up, he performed his ritual ablutions and the pre-dawn prayer and then asked for his shroud. Kissing it, he said, "I eagerly accept my Lord's command." He lay down and passed away.'

Sheikh Abul Hasan al-Shadhili (d. 1275)

He was born in a village called Ghanmara in Morocco. According to custom, he began his education by memorizing the Qur'an, then learning Arabic grammar and Islamic jurisprudence from 'Abd al-Salam ibn Mashish, a local scholar famous for his piety, scrupulousness in religious matters and the dedication of his life to the service of God. He would say, 'the four best states of mind are loving God, contentedness with the Divine decree, renouncing the world and reliance upon God. The four best states of the body are to practise the obligatory duties, to avoid forbidden things, patience and piety.' This great teacher diligently prepared his brilliant student to take on the mantle of Sufism. Upon completing his education, his master instructed him to go to the town of Shadhlah.

As a bright young scholar, al-Shadhili began his teaching and preaching, but soon realized that he had to undergo further spiritual training. Consequently, he began to spend more time on Mount Zaghwan, which was full of physical hardship. He lived on the little the mountain could provide, yet inwardly he found comfort and relief. He devoted himself to worship and following the Sunnah. After spending a considerable time in the wilderness, he decided to leave and head for Tunis, with his heart and mind enlightened and emptied of all except God.

He was welcomed by the public, the scholars and the court in Tunis: people flocked to his lectures to gain inspiration. Handsome and eloquent, he spoke from a pure heart with passion: the love of God overflowed in his discourses. His simple yet elegant lifestyle displayed the Sunnah in all its glory, his devotion was a model of sincerity, and his knowledge was like an ocean. Al-Shadhili then moved to Alexandria, a city of scholars and saints, where his reputation spread quickly and people rushed to listen to his lectures to listen to him. Many scholars of the city pledged allegiance to him, notably Abu al-'Abbas al-Mursi, who became his most famous disciple.

The Sheikh travelled to Makkah to perform the hajj. The highlight of his journey was paying homage to the Chosen One (al-Mustafa) in Madinah. Upon arriving in the city, he went straight to the Prophet's Mosque and stood outside awaiting permission to enter. A voice called out, 'O 'Ali, enter!' The Sheikh went in and stood facing the tomb, and read a long eulogy saying: 'Peace be on you, O Messenger, and God's mercy and blessings. I bear witness, O Messenger, that you delivered what you were sent with, you counselled your nation, worshipped your Lord and you were as the description in the Qur'an, a messenger from amongst his own people, who cannot bear them to suffer difficulties, eager for their welfare and compassionate and merciful to the believers.' The Sunnah was woven in the fabric of the Sheikh's life and he always commanded his followers to adhere strictly to it, for, as our Prophet ﷺ taught us, those who follow his way will not be led astray. The Sheikh also cautioned, 'Beware of the knowledge that comes your way for it is risky and perilous, attractive and enjoyable. Take it only if it is true. Remember, the knowledge revealed to the beloved Messenger ﷺ was the real knowledge, followed by that of the Companions, their Successors and the great teachers that came after them. They were free from whim and caprice. Guard yourself against doubts, weak opinions, superstitions and false claims.'

The Sheikh presented a balanced view of a person's relationship with material things. While many Sufis taught renunciation of the world, abandoning society and material things, he corrected this 'monkish' view. One day his favourite disciple, Abu al-'Abbas al-Mursi, came to him determined to renounce the world and live like a monk. With his spiritual insight, the Sheikh perceived al-Mursi's intentions and said to him, 'O Abu al-'Abbas, recognize God and then live as you wish.' In other words, outward appearance, practice and expression do not determine the value of an act, rather it is recognition of one's Lord and seeking Divine pleasure that really determines its value. He bridged between the outward and the inward and the body and the mind in his teachings. Wearing expensive clothes and eating and drinking delightful food and drink do not carry blame if one truly thanks God. He would say, 'Do not exaggerate renunciation of the world, as hardships will overwhelm you and your bodies will waste away. Go back to it and embrace it thoughtfully and with courage.' Of course, this balanced approach is not be confused with the modern ideology of economic progress that promotes love of the world. This is plunging humanity into a whirlpool of greed and selfishness.

His second great contribution to Islamic thought and revival was his correction of the view about seeking proofs for Divine existence. Ibn Ata'illah sums up the Sheikh's view: 'If the creation does not need proof since it is plainly visible, then it goes without saying that the Creator requires no proof either.' Commenting on this, 'Abd al-Halim Mahmud said, 'This is the true Islamic view, in contrast to the view of the philosophers who talk about proving the existence of God.' The Sheikh presented the true Islamic paradigm for knowing God Almighty, which requires faith in the unseen. He said, 'We should look at God with the eyes of *iman* and that will spare us from seeking proofs.' The Sheikh invited the Muslims back to the original Islamic way of thinking, all this in a time when rationalism was at its peak, and insisted that this Aristotelian way of thinking about God was not only wrong but potentially threatening.

The Sheikh stressed the importance of living a simple life in submission to the Lord as this is the key to spiritual intelligence. Such a life requires strict discipline and control of our whims and caprice. He advised his disciples, 'O brother! You must always do *dhikr*, as it helps save you from the punishment in the world and the Hereafter.' To avoid stress and live in a state of serenity and calmness he urged the adoption of *rida*, contentment with the Divine decree: 'Throw yourself at the door of *rida* and give up your own wishes and desires.'

Sheikh Ahmad Faruqi Sirhindi (d. 1624)

> Whose head did not bow before Emperor Jahangir
> Whose breath inspires the freedom fighters
> The protector of Islam in India
> Who was alerted by the Lord at the right moment

This is how the poet-philosopher Iqbal paid tribute to Sheikh Ahmad Faruqi who was born in 1562 in the town of Sirhind in the East Punjab. His father Sheikh 'Abdul Ahad was a great scholar of his day. He paid special attention to the education of his intelligent son, who later on was sent to Lahore and Sialkot for further studies. His father also initiated him into the Qadiriyyah Sufi order, however, after his father's death, he became the disciple of Khwajah Baqi Billah of Delhi, a leading Naqashbandi sheikh, who once wrote of his disciple: 'In Sirhind is a young man by the name of Ahmad Faruqi who has extensive knowledge and immense willpower. ... I hope he shall prove to be such a shining light that will enlighten the entire world.' Sheikh Ahmad married the daughter of Sheikh Sultan, a nobleman of Thanesar. He used the dowry she brought to build a magnificent mosque in Sirhind. The Sheikh had seven sons all of whom were illustrious Sufis. He made his eldest son Khwajah Ma'sum his chief successor who played an important role in spreading the Naqshbandi order in India.

Sheikh Ahmad made many contributions to strengthening Islam in India: His struggle was against the Emperor Akbar who had formed a new religion (Din-i Ilahi) at his court, a mixture of Hinduism, Islam, Christianity, Jainism and Zoroastrianism. The new religion was an elite cult of personality centred around Akbar (only nineteen high-ranking courtiers joined it). The real issue arose with some of the royal decrees that the Emperor issued to restrict religious practice in the name of tolerance: he promoted the celebration of Nauruz, the prohibition of the common people learning Arabic, the prohibition of eating cows and buffalos, the prohibition of slaughtering animals for up 180 days in each year, the reform of Shariah regulations on marriage and male circumcision, and the burial of the dead with their heads towards the east away from Makkah. Those ulema who strongly opposed Akbar were exiled, and centres of rebellion in Bihar and Bengal had mosques closed and the Qur'ans produced there were destroyed. As he could not tolerate what he saw as Akbar's blatant blasphemy, Sheikh Ahmad challenged the Emperor's new religion and decrees on religious matters for which he was imprisoned.

When Akbar's son Jahangir came to throne, he freed the Sheikh, abolished his father's Din-i Ilahi and restored the practice

Masters

of Shariah. With his release, Sheikh Ahmad began preaching Islam to the troops in the imperial army and to court officials, which had a tremendous impact. The Sheikh was also a prolific writer in particular he wrote letters to disciples and noblemen encouraging them to re-establish Islam.

Hafiz 'Abdul Karim (d.1936)

Affectionately known as Hafizji, Hafiz Muhammad 'Abdul Karim of Rawalpini (b. 1848) was born into a well-respected religious Moghul family, which had originally migrated from Afghanistan. His mother died when he three months old and his father, Nazar Muhammad, a pious Sufi, died when he was two years old. Orphaned, he was taken in and looked after by his uncle Pir Bakhsh and aunt Hayat Bibi with great love and care, who paid special attention to his education and moral and spiritual development. He studied the Qur'an, Hadith and *fiqh* from a local scholar Qadi Muhammad Zaman, and was an exceptional student both academically and in terms of his character. He completed memorization of the Qur'an in thirty months and learnt *tajwid* from the well-known Qari Muhammad Hussayn Makki. Hafizji used to recite the Qur'an in a beautiful and melodious style, which enchanted listeners. He learnt his uncle's craft as a dyer and made this his means of livelihood.

Hafizji would often be recite the glorious Qur'an as he worked in the dye shop. In 1873, at the age of twenty-five, Hafizji visited the great Sufi sheikh Baba Faqir Muhammad at Choora. Babaji saw signs of greatness and spirituality in the young hafiz and immediately took him as a disciple. Captivated by the pious Babaji, the young Hafizji became a devout follower. Over time, as his bond with his Sheikh grew deeper, he withdrew from his worldly activities and began to serve him. Hafizji's inner self underwent a metamorphosis as he spent more time in *dhikr* and less at the workshop. The time came when Babaji made Hafizji his new deputy (*khalifah*), giving him permission to take *bay'ah* of others and guide them. He took his responsibility as a Naqshbandi sheikh very seriously, and spent his entire life until he died at the age of eighty-eight in 1936 in devotion, the service of God and the promotion of the spiritual welfare of all those who came in contact with him.

Hafiz 'Abdul Karim emulated the beloved Messenger's lifestyle in every way and taught his followers about his beautiful character. Kind and gentle, Hafizji never took revenge in spite of being able to do so. He would not become angry if anyone spoke harshly towards him. He greeted people humbly with a smile and spoke sweetly and gently with genuine concern. He never distinguished between rich and poor and respected everyone. His great love for people made each person believe that Hafizji loved him more than anyone else. He visited the sick and attended funeral prayers even if they were far off. His disciple Qadi 'Alim Din gives us an eyewitness account of Hafizji's kindness that one day he saw a heron limping in the courtyard. He caught it, examined its broken leg and bandaged it, feed it with seeds and water and then let it fly away. Some of his disciples remarked that he had let go delicious bird fit for eating. He answered that 'I was disturbed to see the poor creature limping. The Lord had sent him here to be healed.' He also used to say, 'Be kind to every creature for it pleases the Creator.'

Hafizji prayed in congregation, and spent the night in vigil, praying, reciting the glorious Qur'an, and remembering God. He was a living example of the Qur'anic verse: *The angels descend on those who say, 'Our Lord is God' and then are steadfast (Fussilat* 41: 30). A longstanding disciple Qadi 'Alim Din relates that on the death of his two sons, Hafizji lead their funeral prayer but there was no change in his daily routine of worship.

Masters

Hafizji relied on God in every matter with the conviction that the real executor of all worldly affairs is God, and all else – sustenance, receiving and giving, life and death, wealth and poverty, suffering and ease – is His creating. He used to say, 'If a farmer neither ploughs the land nor sows seed but still hopes to gather a harvest, then he is foolish and ignorant of Divine providence'. In order to teach reliance on God (*tawakkul*) he often related that one day Prophet Muhammad ﷺ noticed a Bedouin leaving his camel without tying it and asked him, 'Why don't you tie your camel?' The Bedouin answered, 'I put my trust in God.' The Prophet ﷺ then said, 'Tie your camel first, then put your trust in God.' (Tirmidhi)

Hafizji was most thoughtful, reflective and contemplative and used to encourage his disciples to review every event in their lives and take lessons from it. He used to say that 'A moment's reflection is better than a whole night vigil.' He also led an ascetic lifestyle and abstained from excessive worldly pleasures (*zuhd*) in emulation of the Prophet's way; he used to say, 'Poverty is my pride.' This was not about avoiding benefit from God's bounties, as Hafizji explained *zuhd* as not placing more trust in whatever one possesses than in what God has in His possession.

Hafizji said, 'The diseases of the heart are most dangerous and sadly far too many people are afflicted by them. For every one person with a physical disease there are 999 people with diseases of the heart. Remember! The only people who will be blessed are people with healthy hearts. The symptom of physical illness is a lack of appetite while the symptom of the diseased heart is lack of appetite for Divine remembrance. Just as the body depends on food for survival, the heart depends on the food of Divine remembrance. Tranquillity of heart comes from *dhikr*; its neglect leads to the heart's death.'

Hafizji said, 'To contemplate after the pre-dawn prayer until after sunrise is a sure way to draw closer to God. This is why the Messenger ﷺ said, "Anyone who sits quietly doing *dhikr* until the sun has risen will get the reward of an accepted minor pilgrimage (*'umrah*)." Men of God never waste such opportunities, so, my friends, you must engage in this.'

KEY POINT

❀ Those who are closest to God are His friends, and they devote themselves and their lives to Him and in service to others. They are living examples who teach and inspire us to acquire spiritual intelligence.

Select Bibliography

Abdel-Haleem, M. (trans.), *The Qur'an* (Oxford: University Press, 2005).

Abdul Karim, H., *Journey to God* (Nottingham: The Invitation House, 2006).

Buzan, T., *The Power of Spiritual Intelligence* (London: Thorsons, 2001).

Foster, R., *Celebration of Discipline* (London: Hodder & Stoughton, 2008).

Geldard, R., *The Spiritual Teachings of Rolf Waldo Emerson* (USA: Lindisfarne Books, 2001).

Goleman, D., *Social Intelligence* (London: Random House, 2006).

Hujwiri, *The Kashf al-Mahjub*, translated by R. A. Nicholson (London: Luzac, 1976).

Jessop, T. E., *The Christian Morality* (London: Epworth Press, 1960).

Al-Jilani, 'Abd al-Qadir, *Revelations of the Unseen (Futuh al-Ghayb)*, translated by Muhtar Holland (Houston: Al-Baz Publishing, 1992).

Al-Jilani, 'Abd al-Qadir, *The Path of the Worshipful Servants (Minhaj al- 'Abidin)*, translated by Muhtar Holland (Houston: Al-Baz Publishing, 2011).

Lewis, B., *Music of a Distant Drum* (Princeton: University Press, 2001).

Lings, M., *What is Sufism?* (Lahore: Suhail Academy, 2000).

Nasr, S. H., *The Heart of Islam* (San Francisco: Harper, 2002).

Al-Nawawi, Abu Zakariyah Yahya ibn Sharaf, *Riyad al-Salihin (Gardens of the Righteous)*, 2 vols, translated by S. M. Madni Abbasi (Riyadh: International Islamic Publishing House, 1984).

Panipati, Qadi Muhammad Thanaullah 'Uthmani, *Tafsir Mazhari*, 6 vols (Karachi: Shakil Press, 1999).

Al-Qushayri, *Principles of Sufism*, translated by B.R. von Schegell (USA: Mizan Press, 1990).

Al-Razi, Fakhr al-Din Muhammad ibn 'Umar, *Tafsir al-Kabir*, 32 vols (Cairo, 1938).

Rumi, *The Masnavi*, vols 1–3, translated by Jawid Mojaddedi (Oxford: University Press, 2001–2013).

Al-Shabrawi, 'Abd al-Khaliq, *The Degrees of the Soul*, translated by Mostafa al-Badawi (London: The Quilliam Press, 1997).

Al-Shadhili, 'Abd al-Qadir 'Isa, *Haqa'iq 'an al-Tasawwuf* (N.p.: Dar al-'Irfan, 2006).

Siddiqui, A. R., *Tazkiyah: The Islamic Path of Self-Development* (Markfield: Islamic Foundation, 2004).

ALSO AVAILABLE IN THE SAME SERIES:

Seven Steps to Moral Intelligence
Musharraf Hussain

How do we improve ourselves so that we can live by the universal moral values of Islam? This straightforward guide tells us how to do this in seven steps.

Based on the teachings of Imam al-Ghazali and upon years of practical experience in teaching young Muslims, Dr Musharraf Hussain has given us a contemporary and accessible way to understand and apply Islamic teachings to character building.

£3.99 | Paperback | 108pp
ISBN: 978-1-84774-009-0